COFFEE HOUSE TILES. (*From Spitalfields.*)

See App. G.

EDWARD ROBINSON

THE EARLY ENGLISH COFFEE HOUSE

With an Account of the First Use of Coffee

THE DOLPHIN PRESS
CHRISTCHURCH

First printed 1893
This edition 1972

The Dolphin Press, 176 Barrack Road
Christchurch, Hants.

ISBN 0 85642 005 0

Printed in Great Britain
by Biddles Ltd., Guildford, Surrey

Bound by James Burn at
Esher, Surrey

"The history of coffee houses, ere the invention of clubs, was that of the manners, the morals, and the politics of a people."—*Isaac D'Israeli*.

PREFACE.

THE object of this book is to trace the origin of the
English Coffee House system, and to describe its
part in the social and political life of the seventeenth century.

To the general reader this subject will prove interesting chiefly on account of the glimpse which
it affords into the condition of the common people
at a critical moment in our national history.
Against the misgovernment of the later Stuarts
all opposition seemed in vain. The tactics of Parliamentary parties were frustrated, concessions
and schemes of reconciliation proved abortive, the
Press was no longer a bulwark of public liberty ;
and, as if the country had grown weary of battling
for freedom, the very municipalities were volun-
tarily surrendering their privileges. Great changes
in our constitution were inevitable. That those
changes were in the direction of progress, and that
they took place in time to preserve much of the
old order, was due in part to the fact that the

popular voice found an unlooked-for means of
utterance.   The Coffee House Club, though of
Eastern origin, adapted itself to English social
traditions and assimilated some of the best elements of Puritanism.   Thus invigorated its influence began to be felt when more ancient insti-
tutions seemed temporarily paralyzed.

Only one feature of the new institution need
here be insisted upon.   The Coffee Houses were
without any regular organization.   They were
used for a hundred purposes besides that of political debate, and were frequented by almost every
class in society.   Merchants pursuing their business, those who were in need of refreshment, and
loungers of every description, resorted hither continually.   Literary critics made certain of these
places their haunts ; learned and scientific subjects
were discussed ; and yet more often persons were
to be found here eagerly inquiring about the
gaieties of the town and latest productions at the
theatre.

At first this want of combination, as well as their
simplicity and homeliness, caused the influence of
the Coffee Houses to be undervalued, and when
their importance could no longer be ignored they
were still curiously misunderstood.   Both the

Samuel Pepys and the brave but unfortunate Harrington.

A constant frequenter of Coffee Houses—and one whose name deserves to be rescued from oblivion—was "Master Harry Blunt." His character seemed to contain in miniature stern Puritan elements together with those more genial qualities which rendered the Coffee Houses popular.

Lastly, I have investigated the hitherto neglected claim of the early Coffee House to be considered as a Temperance institution. In order that such descriptions as I have given may not appear exaggerated, it is well to bear in mind that the terms used of the Coffee Houses during the time that Dryden bore rule at Will's are not equally applicable at a later date. The institution was complete, and its distinctive features were already becoming obscured, at a time when particular establishments, such as St. James's and the Bedford, were still increasing in fashionable repute. We are concerned only with the earlier period before the name of Coffee House had become a misnomer, before it had lost anything of its generous social traditions, and whilst the issue of the struggle for political liberty was as yet uncertain.

In the course of my inquiries there has been

occasion to refer to contemporary evidence of all kinds. Newspaper advertisements, reports of trials during the season of the " Popish Plots," Admiralty and Domestic State Papers, including verification of particular points by reference to the original manuscripts, and the important results of the MSS. Commission, have proved as fertile in information as the few treatises professedly dealing with our subject. The early broadsides and pamphlets—a sufficiently numerous class—have received special attention. They are for the most part quoted in the body of the book, and the Bibliography at the end contains a complete list in chronological order. In cases of special interest— e.g. the "Character" of 1665, and some details concerning the " Rota "—and with a view to diminishing the number of the footnotes, it has seemed best to throw into an Appendix extracts that were otherwise too long for quotation.

It only remains to express my hearty thanks for help received.

From the Committee of the Guildhall Library I have obtained permission to procure copies of their valuable collection of Tokens, as well as of the unique Coffee House tiling (a beautiful specimen of seventeenth century workmanship) in the Museum of the Guildhall. The list of Tokens in the Appendix I owe to the courtesy of E. M. Borrajo, Esq., of the Guildhall Library.

I would especially mention the kindness of the Baroness Burdett-Coutts, in permitting free access to an interesting collection of pamphlets and engravings in her possession.

My thanks are due to J. Macfarlane, Esq., of the British Museum, for no small amount of help in the matter of revision ; and to him I am also indebted for having drawn my attention to valuable sources of information.

LIST OF ILLUSTRATIONS.

CONTENTS.

CHAPTER I.

EARLY LEGENDS.

CHAPTER II.

EARLY HISTORY.

CHAPTER III.

ACCOUNTS BY TRAVELLERS.

CHAPTER IV.

MEDICAL HISTORY.

CHAPTER V.

EARLIEST COFFEE HOUSES UNDER THE COMMONWEALTH.

CHAPTER VI.

THE COFFEE HOUSE AS A SOCIAL AND TEMPERANCE FACTOR.

CHAPTER VII.

COFFEE HOUSES UNDER THE STUARTS: THE HOME OF LIBERTY.

CHAPTER VIII.

DEVELOPMENT AND DECLINE.

No. 1.

FARR AT RAINBOW,

FLEET STREET.

No. 2.

MORAT YE GREAT,

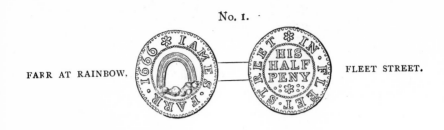

EXCHANGE ALLEY.

No. 3.

UNION,

CORNHILL.

No. 4.

SULTANESS,

SWEETINGS RENTS.

See pp. 146-8 and App. G.

THE EARLY HISTORY OF COFFEE HOUSES.

CHAPTER I.

EARLY LEGENDS.

"They will ask thee concerning wine."—*Koran.*

"THAT part of Araby the Blessed which is called Yemen the Happy"—such is the name of the country, according to Mohammedan tradition, where the uses of coffee were first made known to "The Faithful."

There exist three distinct accounts, which are interesting not for their historical value, but as showing how from the very outset partisans of coffee were anxious to give to their beverage religious associations and connect its use with names of happy import. Whilst the first of these begins by narrating a series of miracles, it is worth noticing that the remaining part of the story would be complete by itself, and is in fact related in a Turkish version without any such introduction.

We may therefore conclude that in the following narrative a real adventure has been tacked on to a fragment from the life of the patron saint and legendary founder of Mocha, which in its turn may be a Mohammedan rendering of some still older original.

" Here," says Abd-alkader Ansari-djezeri, " is an account of the manner in which coffee was discovered.[1]   In the year of the Hegira 656 [Jan. 8, 1258—Nov. 29, 1258 A.D.] the Sheikh Abou'l hasan Schadhéli, whilst journeying by Sewaken [Suakim], on pilgrimage to Mecca, said to his disciple, the Sheikh Omar, when he had come to the mountain of Êbrek. . . . 'I shall die in this place.   When I have delivered up my spirit, you must perform everything commanded by a certain person whom you will see coming ; moreover he will have his face covered with a veil.'   Shortly after the death of the Sheikh (Schadhéli) the person whom he had foretold actually appeared, having his face covered, and dug down ever so little in the same place.   Immediately water appeared by the permission of God : the Sheikh Omar

---

[1] See " Chrestomathie arabe," edited by Silvestre de Sacy, where the above is quoted from M. Armain's translation of " Géographe turc."

helped himself to some of the water." The ghost of his teacher, for such it was, presently left him, but not before giving careful instructions to carry the water, which had just appeared in such marvellous manner, in a bowl; and further, it bade him notice exactly where the water in the bowl ceased to move to and fro, for on that spot was he to take up his abode. Accordingly the Sheikh travelled forward until he had reached Mocha by sea—when he landed, the water in the bowl ceased to move. Moreover, a supply of fresh water appeared in that place, though this was the first spring of the kind known in the city.

This wonderful water proved not to be his chief discovery, and just as the traveller seemed to have reached the goal he entered afresh upon a new sea of trouble, in order, as it were, to connect himself with our subject. His skill as a doctor was acknowledged in the city, but his moral repute came under a cloud and the accused was forced to retire into exile. In his retreat at Ousab he was sought out by certain citizens from Mocha, who were now in sore need of his medical aid. Meanwhile the Sheikh and his companions had felt the stress of poverty, and were reduced to feeding upon the berries that grew around them; and thus, in the words of our Arab narrator, having "nothing to eat except coffee, they took of it and boiled it in a saucepan and drank of the decoction." The Sheikh was not slow to see that what had already saved himself and his followers from death by starvation might prove beneficial in less critical cases ; accordingly the visitors from Mocha were dosed with the only physic which he now possessed. They returned full of the praises of the newly-found medicine and of its fortunate discoverer.

The result is seen in a triumphant return of the Sheikh to the city of Mocha, where he is welcomed by the now reconciled governor, and a monastery is built and fitted up for the reception of himself and his followers.

It sometimes happens that a patient who has long been accustomed to a particular medicine is unwilling or unable to give it up when its use is no longer required. Nor does this occur only where the physic is an alcoholic stimulant. The good people of Mocha, both doctor and patients, were fully agreed that coffee should be continued as a beverage.

The Sheikh was not now in danger of starving, and the citizens were no longer ailing ; but what had once been so needful for the prolonging of life

was found to be equally indispensable for the comfort of existence. Coffee, as we should nowadays
express it, became a needful luxury.

Another version of this tradition, being the
one derived from a Turkish source, comes to us
in the following manner. In the year 1683, says
M. Victor Tissot,[1] when the city of Vienna was
surrounded and hard pressed by a Turkish army,
one of the besieged offered his services to the
governor. Having assumed a Mohammedan disguise, he went forth to act as a spy, and presently
returned with the joyful news that succour was at
hand and the enemy were about to retire. Being
asked to name his own reward for these tidings,
he only requested permission to carry away the
innumerable bags left behind by the Turks in
their flight, whilst to the wondering governor he

---

[1] The hero, Kalezyski, was presented with a house by the
grateful municipality, and here, at the sign of "The Blue
Bottle," he continued as coffee-man for many years. This
tale is in part confirmed by a contemporary "Relation of the
Siege of Vienna" (1684, John Peter a Valcaren), where one
Geo. Kotschkitsky is mentioned as passing through the
enemy's ranks in the disguise of a merchant. In another
account he is named "Francis Kotchizki alias Kotlenski."
The Librarian at Vienna informs me that the story of the
bags of coffee, and of permission granted to open a coffee
house, is not authenticated, though "seriously related in
many books and firmly believed throughout Vienna."

explained that these contained the secret of a
drink discovered by accident in the manner already
described.   His story of the Sheikh differs a little
as to details, and, what is remarkable, omits all
mention of the holy water in the bowl.   It is
added that the Sheikh first tried coffee raw,
and, finding it bitter, the lucky idea occurred to
bake and then boil the berry.[1]

The second account of the finding of the berry
is a yet more simple story from which the element
of miracle is entirely absent.   " A certain person,"
we are told, " who looked after camels (or goats, as
others report, which last is the common tradition
among the people of the East) complained to the
Religious of a neighbouring monastery in the land
of Ayaman (i.e., Arabia Felix) that his herds twice
or thrice a week not only kept awake all the night,
but spent it in frisking and dancing in an unusual
manner.   The Prior of the monastery, led by his
curiosity to weigh the matter seriously, concluded
this must happen from what the creatures fed
upon.   Marking therefore diligently that very

---

[1] Sir Hans Sloane (Phil. Trans., 1694) says the husks are
often dried in the sun instead of being baked by fire, and
" the Arabians themselves in summer heats use these husks
roasted after the manner of coffee-berries, esteeming that
drink more cooling, it being sourish to the taste."

night, in company with one of his monks, the place where the goats or camels pastured when they danced, he found there certain shrubs or bushes, on the fruit or rather berries of which they fed. He resolved to try the virtues of these berries himself, and accordingly boiling them in water and drinking the liquor, he found by experience that it kept him awake in the night." Now the worthy Prior was not the man to keep such a discovery to himself, and we find that " ever afterwards he enjoined the daily use of it to his monks, which, by keeping them from sleep, made them more readily and surely attend the devotions that they were obliged to perform in the night time."

The wonder of the wakeful monastery soon attracted notice : the marvellous berry " came to be in request throughout the whole kingdom, and in progress of time other nations and provinces of the East fell into the use of it."

The simplicity of the tale is marred when Banesius, writing in the seventeenth century, solemnly introduces it by a long paragraph upon the " virtues that lie concealed in stones, minerals, plants, and animals." Moreover, this is not the only excellent medicine of which the use has been revealed by chance, or taught us by the brute creation ; we have the dictamnus for drawing out arrows which deer first showed to men ; the wild boars heal their maladies with ivy ; the weasel in his conflicts with the adder is indebted to rue for his cure ; wild marjoram is the stork's physic; the hippopotamus, who of purpose wounds himself in the thigh and heals the hurts with slimy mud, first showed us the use and operation of letting blood, &c., &c. [1]

With the same grave air of persuasion Banesius informs us that the Turks themselves acknowledge their indebtedness to the Christians, " being wont to own that these monks were the inventors (of this liquor), and in a sort of thankfulness and gratitude to those monks, when serving or handing the

[1] Faustus Nairo Banesius in his letter (written in Latin) to the Cardinal Nic. de Comitibus (in 1671), is the first to record this tradition. For the above paragraph, cf. Bacon, "Advancement of Learning" (Bk. V. ch. ii.), where the Æneid is quoted to show that the use of dittany was learnt from the wild goat, also that we are indebted to the accidental flying off of a pot's cover for artillery. With regard to the instinct of brutes, he asks, Who taught the parrot its "good-morrow"? Who instructed the raven, in a drought, to drop pebbles into a hollow tree, where she chanced to spy water, that the water might rise for her to drink? Another equally "grave introduction" is quoted from M. du Four by Dr. J. Douglas in the " History of the Coffee Tree." Moseley's "Treatise on Coffee" (1785) gives a version of the tradition, but Douglas's translation (1727) has been followed as being more faithful.

liquor, they are used to pray in set forms of oraisons for Sciadli and Aidrus, which they believe were the names of the Prior and his companions."

The tradition comes to us without date and without authority, and it would be impossible to say that its two monks were not the "Religious" of a certain Mohammedan order to whom we shall have occasion to refer. In any case the obligation, if it ever existed, has been liberally cancelled, for it is to Mohammed's teaching in the Koran that the world indirectly owes whatever of good has resulted from the discovery of the uses of coffee.

At first sight we might suppose that the "Bible of the Mohammedans" could have nothing whatever to do with our subject. Composed as it was in moments of rhapsody, which according to some of Mohammed's apologists may be resolved into epileptic fits, his "Revelation" included a miscellany of orders for the day, directions to the faithful concerning the manifold duties of life, and copious warnings against all who rejected the prophet's mission. Yet amongst the list of its varied contents comes the well-known prohibition of wine.

Of three passages which refer to the subject, one

seems to admit a double interpretation, for the prophet declares " of the fruit of palm-trees and grapes ye obtain inebriating drinks, and also good nourishment." The second has been sometimes urged in favour of a moderate indulgence (so to speak) in the forbidden fruit. We read as follows in the second chapter :—

"They will ask thee concerning wine and lots : Answer, In both there is great sin, and *also some* things of use unto men ; but their sinfulness is greater than their use."

The third passage allows no loophole of escape : lotteries, together with all such appeals to chance, and, it is said, even the innocent game of chess on account of its little wooden figures, are therein forbidden :—

"Oh, true believers, surely wine and lots, and images, and divining arrows, *are* an abomination of the work of Satan ; therefore avoid them that ye may prosper. Satan seeketh to sow dissension and hatred among you, by means of wine and lots, to divert you from remembering God and from prayer : will ye not therefore abstain *from them ?* "[1]

The faithfulness with which the true sons of Moslem obeyed this injunction gave rise to earnest inquiry whether or no there might exist a substitute free from the intoxicating effects, and yet able

---

[1] Geo. Sale's Translation of the Koran, 5th edit., pp. 25 and 93 ; see also his *Introduction.*

in some sort to supply the stimulating pleasures of wine.

To this question the finding and adoption of the coffee drink was an answer which at first seemed complete, but was afterwards thought too good to be true.

Curiously enough the word for coffee in Arabia was exactly the same as one of those employed for wine, and this coincidence was used to support an argument that the prohibition in the Koran applied to both alike. The partisans of coffee so far admitted the difficulty as to suggest that the name should be altered from Kahavah to Kirwah. It was also urged by way of distinction that whereas Kahwah meant literally *loathing* or *distaste*, this in the case of wine was to be referred to food, whilst by the drinkers of coffee the disinclination was felt for sleep. The Koran had forbidden all assembling for the purpose of drinking wine, and though it was allowed that Mohammed himself had sat in company in order to partake of milk from a bowl, it was argued by unreasoning zealots that the social assemblages at which coffee was drunk might be included under the ban.

Equally futile was the endeavour of the partisans of coffee to show that even if Mohammed himself was unacquainted with the beverage (though there is a tradition that it was supplied to the prophet by the hand of the angel Gabriel), yet he had in the sacred book foretold its adoption by the faithful, saying,—

"They shall be given to drink an excellent wine, sealed; its seal is that of the musk."

A reference to this passage will be found amongst the early Arab verses of which we are about to give a translation; indeed it may be said that the whole attempt of the later Mohammedans to read the word "coffee" into their Koran belongs rather to the region of poetry than history, as do similar attempts to find it in the Bible and the classics.

Since in the time of Mohammed, who flourished in the seventh century of our Christian Era, its use was as yet undiscovered in Arabia, we may fairly conclude that coffee was unknown to the ancients; nor need we be at pains to consider whether or no "it is a great presumption against the antiquity of a custom that we find no footsteps of it in ancient monuments."

An English rhymester of the seventeenth century bids us go look for the virtues of coffee in prose, "for it cannot stand in verse." Another tells how the poets have agreed in lofty strains:

> To praise the (now too frequent) use
> Of the bewitching grape's strong juice,

and pleads, in excuse for ten pages of doggerel, the poverty of a subject so ill-suited to higher flights of imagination :

> Only poor coffee seems to me
> No subject fit for poetry.

A third is even more emphatic, though he joins the refusal with a handsome compliment :

> To raise our coffee in a verse or two,
> Is more than all the peopled world can do :
> Whose rare transcendent Virtues so extend
> It cannot be within a poem penn'd.

Yet, as there was to the Eastern mind no such divorce between our subject and poetry, we have from the Arabian manuscript a fair number of verses in praise of the berry, composed by distinguished men of letters and by recluses in high repute for sanctity. A few of the lines on account of their quaintness are set before the reader as specimens :

Oh coffee ! thou dost scatter all our cares, thou the object of the vows of him who devotes himself to study.

The beverage of the friends of the Holy, it imparts health to those of his servants who toil to acquire wisdom.

A drink innocent as the pure milk, differing therefrom but in its dark colour.

Delicious drink, whose colour is the seal that answers to its purity.

'Tis a *wine* which no care could possibly resist when the
　　cup-bearer presents it.

Whoso has once known the warmth . . . has henceforth
　　only aversion for wine and the liquor of the casks.[1]

The following rhymes by La Roque are adapted
from a prose translation of an original Turkish
sonnet. In an English version of this author they
are omitted, doubtless as being unable to sustain a
further process of translation, and this must be my
excuse for giving them here in the French :

> A Damas, Alep, au grand Caire,
> Il s'est promené tour à tour,
> Ce doux fruit, qui fournit une boisson si chere,
> Avant que de venir triompher à la Cour.
> Là ce seditieux, perturbateur du monde,
> A par sa vertu sans seconde,
> Supplanté tous les vins depuis cet heureux jour.

---

[1] For the following rendering I am indebted to a friend :

Oh coffee ! loved and fragrant drink, thou drivest care away,
The object thou of that man's wish who studies night and
　　day,
Thou soothest him, thou giv'st him health, and God doth
　　favour those
Who walk straight on in wisdom's ways, nor seek their own
　　repose.
Fragrant as musk thy berry is, yet black as ink in sooth !
And he who sips thy fragrant cup can only know the truth.
Insensate they who tasting not yet vilify its use,
For when they thirst and seek its help, God will the gift
　　refuse.
Oh coffee is our wealth ! for see, where'er on earth it grows
Men live whose aims are noble, true virtues who disclose.

CHAPTER II.

EARLY HISTORY.

" Its opponents have hazarded a number of one-sided
opinions."—*Arabian MS.*

AN English writer in the current edition of the
" Encyclopædia Britannica," who warns us against
what he severely calls " an unusual profusion
of conjectural statements and purely mythical
stories," goes on to say that " according to
a statement contained in a manuscript belonging to the Bibliothèque Nationale in Paris, the
use of coffee was known at a period so remote
as 875 A.D., or exactly 1000 years ago." Now
this would at once bring us back to a date
nearly four hundred years earlier than that which,
as we have seen, legend itself is able to offer. The
simple fact that the Arabic manuscript reckons not
according to the Christian era, but from the Hegira
or Flight of Mohammed, at once saves its credit
and takes us down to 1470 A.D. (875 A.H.) for what
may be styled the earliest reliable date in the
History of Coffee.

The document in question has for its title, "The
Strongest Proofs in favour of the lawfulness of the
use of Coffee, by the Sheikh Abd-alkader Ansari
Djezeri." The date of this work is given by De
Sacy as 996 A.H. [i.e. Dec. 2, 1587—Oct. 22, 1588
A.D.].

In the first chapter we have what seems to be a
trustworthy account of the introduction of the
berry into Aden. This is the writer who, in
another work, has preserved the legend of the
Sheikh and bowl, but in the present instance he
confines himself to less wonderful narrations, and,
being content to leave unsettled the question of
the original discovery of coffee, even allows that
for a knowledge of the use of their own berry the
Arabians are indebted to a foreign country.

There is one disadvantage, inasmuch as his
account is taken at second-hand from a writer who
in his turn picked up the story in Egypt ; but this
drawback does not affect us seriously : since we
know practically nothing of these Arabian literati,
one name is as good as another for our purpose.
Here then is what he has to say of "a man whom
science and religion have rendered famous, the
Sheikh, the very learned Imam, the mufti skilled
in the art of ruling, Djemal-eddin Aben Abdallah

Mohammed Bensaid [surnamed from his native village, Aldhabhani]." This worthy being obliged, for some reason or other, to betake himself from Aden into the land of Adjam (i.e. Abyssinia, rendered by some Persia), stayed there long enough to observe that the inhabitants made use of coffee, though he did not at that time acquaint himself fully with its properties. When he returned to Aden he suddenly became ill, and, having bethought himself of coffee, he drank it, and derived much benefit : he noticed, amongst other good qualities, that it had a peculiar power of dispelling all sleep and drowsiness, so that the body was rendered nimble and active. As these effects endeared it to himself, so they suggested the idea of trying it upon his monks, and the results were such as those already described in the case of the wakeful monastery. The story is confirmed by the recollections of an aged man, who says : "I was in the town of Aden when there came thither a monk of the order of the Fakirs, who used to make coffee and drink it himself." The monk quoted in defence of his practice the authority of two doctors, of whom one was the renowned Imam, named by him Dhabhani. Now the Imam, who, in Mohammedan phrase, was advanced in the knowledge of the

Highest, died in the year 875 (1470 A.D.). "You may know by this," says our author, "the period of the introduction of coffee;" he adds, however, that coffee may have been drunk in Aden at an earlier period, and merely sanctioned by the authority of this great name. It is, indeed, a matter for surprise that we have here the first reliable date in the history of our subject, and that coffee drinking, now so universal, can be traced back no further than the middle of the fifteenth century.

When once the thing became fashionable it was adopted throughout the city by learned lawyers, artists, and mechanics, who each and all took coffee with a view to being assisted in their various callings.

Nor was the custom long confined to a corner of Arabia. It had spread ere the close of the century from Aden to Mecca and Medina, passing over to Grand Cairo in Egypt. Here it was that the above story of Aden monks was picked up, and our author says with regard to the introduction of coffee into Egypt, that it came first into a part of Cairo in which certain monks from Yemen had mosques :

"Those who made use of it were the fakirs, who, according to their monastic rule . . . are bound to the recital of certain prayers, and to accomplish the singing of the praises of God. They placed it in a large red earthen vessel; into which their Superior dipped a small bowl and presented some to each of them in turn, beginning with those who were on his right hand, they in the meantime chanting their regular prayers, which most generally consisted of this form: There is no god but one God, the true King, and Whose power is not to be disputed."

The bowl was now freely handed round, and the laymen, in fact all who had assembled to assist in their services, drank it in company with them. Presently the usage grew to be inseparably connected with their worship, so that "they never even performed a religious ceremony in public and never observed any solemn festival without taking coffee."

All these stories, like the earlier legends, agree in attributing to monks and monasteries the first use of the berry; their religious colouring being due in part, at least, to the controversy which just at this time arose. That discussion, as we have already seen, turned for the most part upon Mohammedan law, and our Arabian author sums up in favour of coffee as follows:

"Its opponents . . . have hazarded a number of . . . one-sided opinions which have led . . . to disputes and unhappiness as well at Mecca as at Cairo. The sale of coffee has been forbidden. The vessels used for this beverage, and containing nothing but what was innocent and proper, have been broken to pieces. The dealers in coffee have received the bastinado, and have undergone other ill-treatment without even a plausible excuse ; they were punished by loss of their money. The husks of the plant, from which this liquor is extracted, have been more than once devoted to the flames, and in several instances persons making use of it in view of some bodily or intellectual advantage have been severely handled. On both sides stupidity has been imposed upon : troops of evil spirits and passions which are never about any good have been roused in the Mussulmans."

Nor did this frenzied zeal stop short of downright fanaticism, and there were some who distinctly taught that the injurious effects of coffee would remain even after death. Gloomy strictness occasioned more questionable practices, and there were doubtless many to sympathize with the " man of pleasure " who muttered, " Wine of the bonn (i.e. from the coffee plant) has been refused ; we'll now take freely wine of the raisin." Another in his verses encouraged men of sense to laugh at the intemperate attacks, saying : " Let them alone to beat the water."

It has often been observed that the violence of the controversialist is inversely proportional to the justice of his cause. Pretenders to learning only add to the confusion of the simple by their sophistry and evenly-balanced arguments. The opinion of the well informed is not heeded in a Babel, for "the words of the wise are heard in silence." So the final decision must come from an outsider, in whose case the dictates of common sense are backed by authority. Such, at all events, was the history of the discussion upon the merits of coffee. In order to see how the civil arm at length decided what had been too hard a question for the learned doctors of Mecca, it will be necessary to glance at the bond of political connexion which linked Egypt to Arabia.

For some two centuries and a half there had existed at Grand Cairo a race of Arab kings called the Fatimites, who, as their name implies, claimed a descent and authority derived from Mohammed himself. For a longer period no prince of Arab blood had reigned in Egypt, yet, the old intercourse between the two countries being maintained, the Governor of Mecca was still in the year 1511 A.D. subordinate to the ruler at Cairo.

Khair Beg, Governor of Mecca, was, according to his enemies, unscrupulous to a degree in obtaining money, over careful to perform his duties as a religious censor, and all too ignorant of the condition of the people under his charge.[1] Though

---

[1] For this part of the subject our Arabic author, so often quoted and even misquoted, is still the chief authority: a

presently learning how much coffee was in vogue at Mecca, and that merry-makings at the public coffee-houses were of frequent occurrence, yet he was indebted to an accident for his first knowledge of the popular taste.   One evening when returning from prayers, his astonishment was great on beholding in a corner of the Mosque a group of persons partaking of some unknown liquor, which, his suspicions being aroused, was at once supposed to be wine ; nor was he much relieved by an account of the marvellous virtues of the new drink, and his stern sense of propriety was shocked on finding that those who, unlike himself, spent the whole night at their devotions, were about to fortify themselves in the comfortable manner already described.

The Governor acted with promptness, for he drove the offenders out of the Mosque, and on the morrow summoned a large assembly, including officers of justice, learned doctors of the law, devotees and other principal inhabitants of Mecca. He himself opened the meeting with an account of what was practised in the coffee houses of the

quaint English translation by Dr. Douglas (taken from the French of Antoine Galland) has been freely used in the following pages.

town, and, before asking their opinion, gave it to be clearly understood that he was determined to rectify these abuses.

The doctors of the law were naturally enough not quite ready to decide at a moment's notice that the drink was deserving of condemnation upon religious grounds. They agreed that the coffee houses stood in need of reformation, that things were often done there contrary to the law, and they finally admitted that supposing coffee to be amongst the number of indifferent things, yet, since the use of it occasioned such enormities, it was safest for Mussulmans to hold it unlawful. But they were quite willing to shift their responsibility on to the shoulders of the physicians of the body.

Now the Governor was himself under the influence of Shems-eddin, his confessor, and was by this person persuaded that the evil effects which vulgar fame attributed to coffee were really to be dreaded. Accordingly it was agreed on all sides that the physicians should be consulted in the matter. There seems, by the way, to have been something more than the usual amount of wire-pulling at this early public meeting. The physicians summoned to represent the faculty, two brothers called Hakimani (the two doctors), natives of Persia, were, without a doubt, acknowledged to be the ablest in Mecca, though it is added that their skill consisted more in dialectics than in physic. One of these was already so far committed on the subject that he had written a book against the use of coffee, and must have regarded the opportunity as very excellent by way of advertisement; our author even suggesting that this book was originally penned with a view to check the sale of a liquor so prejudicial to the trade which he drove in physic. They both assured the assembly that the plant bonn (from which coffee was made) was injurious to the health, being, in the language of the famous Aristotelian category, amongst the number of things *frigida et sicca*, cold and dry.

Nor was there wanting a further proof of their skill in learned disputation. When a doctor declared that Bengiazaleh, an ancient and much-respected physician who lived about the time of Avicenna, had said that the bonn was scorching, and that therefore it could not be cold, they replied, perhaps truly, that this was another plant of the same name, though of different virtues.

The advocates of coffee had been completely

taken by surprise, and were accordingly at a disadvantage ; yet for one moment it seemed that a
check would be put upon the eagerness of mistaken
zealots. The mufti was an officer whose religious
authority amongst the Mohammedans was especially sacred. Somewhat later on it happened at
Constantinople that this personage was opposed to
the use of coffee, and none daring to speak against
his decision, the public coffee houses were closed
until the days of a more compliant successor.
On this occasion, however, the poor mufti of
Mecca, pleading earnestly against the hasty decision, though his opinion could not be ignored in
the assembly, found himself heartily abused for
independence of spirit.

The meeting was by this time fully convinced
and ready with true oriental promptness to exercise the functions of a Court of Justice. Some
admitted that their senses had been disordered by
drinking coffee. One, who might be regarded as
permanently affected, actually made the statement that it intoxicated like wine. Thereupon
a general laugh ensued, as it was evident that
he had tasted of both liquors contrary to the
precepts of his religion. Not having the skill to
get out of this admission, he was there and then

condemned to suffer his punishment, viz. the bastinado.

Such was the first public condemnation of coffee. The sentence was rigorously carried out. Officers of Justice were sent into all quarters of the town to shut up coffee houses and burn all the coffee they could lay their hands upon. Some there were who yet ventured to disobey in private, and gladly they quoted in their favour the opinion of the mufti ; but one of these being caught in the act was first treated with some harshness, and was then led through all the public places of the city, mounted upon an ass.

Neither the insolence nor the triumph of the successful party lasted for long. The Governor of Mecca had despatched a letter to his sovereign lord at Cairo, giving an account of his proceedings in the matter. Doubtless the reply caused him unlimited surprise. The prohibition was to be recalled and the authority of the Governor to be again employed, but this time only in preventing the abuse and irregularities of the coffee houses.

Nay, the drink itself was honoured with a comparison, which to the reader of the letter must have seemed little short of profane. Within the great Mosque at Mecca were sacred waters, to partake of which was accounted an act of devotion and one likely to produce happy consequences. These were the miraculous waters of Zem Zem, the same in Mohammedan fancy as the fountain revealed to Hagar in the wilderness. Now the best things might be abused, " as, for example, coffee and the waters of Zem Zem," but this should not make either to be accounted the less proper for use.

Whether or not the Governor was duly impressed by such a reference, he saw good reason to obey the peremptory orders of his master.

The cruelty of the persecutors was presently repaid with something more than poetical justice. As a punishment for what the Governor at Mecca had done against that harmless liquor, the Egyptian ruler " caused him to be put to death about a year after, his concussions and publick robberies being detected." The sad end of the two physicians brings us down to the time when Egypt had been conquered by the Turkish Emperor Selim I. They had indeed left Mecca with the loss of all their reputation upon the reopening of the coffee houses. We might easily forgive their opposition to the Turkish invader in Cairo; but it was an evil fate that pursued the unfortunate brothers, so that " for imprecations and other treasonable words they had uttered against him " he caused them both to be slain.

At Mecca the dispute was very nearly ended. The coffee houses were during a short time closed by order of the Chief Justice of the town, and re-opened under his successor. Once again the drink itself was forbidden by an order from the Emperor at Constantinople, but it was generally known that the prohibition was due to the stratagems of a Court lady, who had only heard of the beverage from pilgrims and other travellers. As the authority of the Turk had been but recently set up in Arabia, so perhaps the loyal inhabitants of Mecca were allowed a certain choice before yielding their obedience to any particular command, and this one they elected entirely to disobey.

In Cairo the question was reopened by a meddlesome doctor, who proposed the following case of conscience :

" What is your opinion concerning the liquor call'd coffee . . . which is drank in all public companies, as a thing that may be freely used ? . . . Is it permitted or is it forbidden ? "

Sending this round to his brethren of the law, he, with commendable foresight, added his own opinion, viz. that " the use of coffee is unlawful." The document proved a testimonial in favour of the contrary opinion, as the other doctors, one and all, failed to ratify this foregone conclusion.

When some ten years later a preacher was so succesful in stirring up the mob by his rhetoric, that they broke into coffee houses and maltreated the company, this question was once more hotly debated. The Chief Justice summoned to a consultation all the doctors of the town. This time the learned showed no hesitation ; they protested that, their opinion having been already recorded, it only remained to curb the impertinence of the zealots and the indiscretion of ignorant preachers.

The judge, foreseeing that his example would be more effective than a lengthened discourse, himself took coffee in the midst of the assembly, and bade them follow his example. Some few years later a company of people were found at a coffee house during the night time, and, being committed to prison, on the next day suffered the bastinado. But as this occurrence took place during the fast of Ramadan (the Mohammedan Lent, though not so strictly observed after sunset) it did not in any way affect the drinking of coffee in its lawful time and season.

With the close of this early discussion we have

completed that chapter in the history of coffee which relates to its discovery and the religious notions that at one time seemed to favour, and then so nearly prevented, its general adoption. To the Mohammedans we may ascribe the credit of finding out coffee, though, like Saturn of old, they showed no sort of tenderness to what might full well be styled their infant Jupiter.

CHAPTER III.

ACCOUNTS BY TRAVELLERS.

" It is accounted a great curtesie amongst them to give
unto their frends when they come to visit them, a finion or
Scudella of Coffa, which is more holesome than toothsome,
for it causeth good concoction and driveth away drowsinesse."
Biddulph.

WE now enter upon a fresh stage in our story.
No longer confined to obscure native writings, we
have before us reports by Europeans of repute,
and in particular by such travellers as Bernier,
Thevenot, and Tavernier ; of these three—as Hallam states in his " Literature of Europe "—the
French may justly boast. Their notices of our
subject are always interesting, though sometimes
careless and incomplete. By most travellers, including a few of our own countrymen, coffee, with
its social customs, was merely regarded as an
amusing Turkish vagary ; yet it is curious to see
how these accounts influenced later opinion, and
in how many respects the early Eastern coffee
house was an exact prototype of the institution
as it afterwards existed in Europe.

It was not until a late period that the more frequent use of the Cape route led to explorations in Arabia itself. This country has almost exclusively occupied our attention hitherto, and we must be content with noticing briefly how La Roque's account of a French expedition, sent thither in 1711, confirms what has been said in the preceding chapters. The party, upon reaching Yemen, were honoured with an invitation to visit the native sovereign, who is described as being independent of all other princes, though his authority was not hereditary. The belief of the inhabitants that their country was the sole producer of coffee was shared by their ruler, and is well illustrated by the following anecdote:

"There was nothing remarkable in the King's Gardens, except the great pains taken to furnish it with all the kinds of trees that are common in the country ; amongst which there were coffee trees, the finest that could be had. When the deputies represented to the King how much that was contrary to the custom of the Princes of Europe (who endeavour to stock their gardens chiefly with the rarest and most uncommon plants that can be found) the King returned them this answer : That he valued himself as much upon his good taste and generosity as any Prince in Europe ; the coffee tree, he told them, was indeed common in his country, but it was not the less dear to him upon that account; the perpetual verdure of it pleased him extremely ; and also the thoughts of its producing a fruit which was nowhere else to be met with ; and when he made a present of that that came from his own Gardens, it was a great satisfaction to him to be able to say that he had planted the trees that produced it with his own hands." [1]

A claim has been put forward in favour of Persia as the fatherland of coffee, and that country will next claim our attention for awhile. Certainly at an early date the coffee house was established as an institution in its chief towns. Moreover, we see in this far Eastern land difficulties, which afterwards proved such a stumbling-block in the path of timid or cautious rulers, boldly encountered and easily overcome.

Of the famous coffee house in Ispahan, we are told that the wife of Shah Abbas, observing great numbers of Persians to resort thither daily and indulge in heated discussion of State affairs, appointed an officer (called a Mollah) to sit there at an early hour every day and entertain the tobacco whiffers and coffee quaffers with some point of law, history, or poetry. This, of necessity, kept

[1] Douglas' Coffee Tree, I. p. 14. This was the second of two French expeditions, Louis XIV. being anxious to effect a settlement for trade. During the stay of the French officers an embassy arrived from the Grand Seignior with the object of persuading the Prince of Yemen not to allow Europeans the right of exporting coffee directly by the Red Sea.

politics in the background ; but so far were the habitués of the coffee house from showing any resentment, that they were wont to regale the mollah with such material comforts as the place provided, and when, on the conclusion of the harangue, he gave notice for all men to go about their business, they cheerfully complied.

Another glimpse at the Persian coffee houses seems ludicrously to anticipate the days when Dryden and Addison would occupy the seat of honour, and bear sway over the realm of letters. Here was the literary potentate duly enthroned and provided with his mock sceptre, so that a traveller tells of "the great diversions made in their coffee houses by their poets and historians, who are seated in a high chair, from whence they make speeches and tell satirical stories, playing in the meantime with a little stick, and the same gestures as our jugglers and legerdemain men do in England." [1]

[1] Olearius was ambassador from the Duke of Holstein to Muscovy and Persia from 1633-9. His travels were first published in German, 1647, see Hallam's "Literature of Europe," sec. iv. ch. xxvi. The above extract, as also Tavernier's description of Ispahan, is taken from "The Natural History of Coffee," 1682. For the quotations from Niebuhr which follow, see translation by Heron, p. 266, and Pinkerton's Voyages, vol. x. p. 196.

Niebuhr's general description of the Arabian,
Syrian, and Egyptian coffee houses, as they existed
in his own day, is somewhat similar.   They are,
says this accurate observer, commonly large halls,
having their floors spread with mats and illumi-
nated at night by a multitude of lamps.   Being
"the only theatres for the exercise of profane
eloquence," and because the Arabians never
engage in any game, poor scholars attend here
to amuse the people.   Select portions are read,
e.g. the adventures of Rustan Sal, a Persian
hero.   Some aspire to the praise of invention, and
compose tales and fables.   They walk up and
down as they recite, or, "assuming oratorical consequence," harangue upon subjects chosen by
themselves.   In one coffee house at Damascus an
orator was regularly hired to tell his stories at a
fixed hour ; in other cases he was more directly
dependent upon the taste of his hearers, as at the
conclusion of his discourse, whether it had consisted of literary topics or of loose and idle tales, he
looked to the audience for a voluntary contribu-
tion.   At Aleppo, again, there was a man with a
soul above the common, who, being a person of
distinction, and one that studied merely for his
own pleasure, had yet " gone the round of all the

coffee houses in the city to pronounce moral harangues."

The favoured land of Ethiopia (roughly corresponding to Abyssinia of to-day) was a term of some indefiniteness amongst the ancients. Here the gods were content to feast, and to forget for awhile the joys of Olympus. In accordance with similar suggestions, put forth seriously by modern writers, we might venture to suppose that it was nectar in the form of coffee which detained these heavenly visitors among "the blameless Ethiopians." Somewhat more capable of proof is a statement, noticed in our last chapter, to the effect that coffee was known to the Ethiopians before its introduction into Arabia. According to Niebuhr, what renders these tales of travellers more probable is the fact "that the fruit of the wild coffee tree is in Arabia so bad as to be unfit for use." Poncet, writing in 1698, maintained that though coffee was in his time little planted in Ethiopia, being only found as a curiosity in gardens, yet it was originally a native of the country. Of this, and of a similar suggestion concerning a shrub found in Bourbon, Dr. Douglas says that they were botanically different to the genuine Arabian coffee plant.

For the history of coffee in Turkey more voluminous material is available.   It is generally supposed that the Turks received the beverage through
the Arabians, just as they adopted from them the
Mohammedan religion.   In the year 1554 A.D.
two persons named Schems and Hekim, coming
the one from Damascus and the other from Aleppo,
are said to have opened the first coffee houses in
Constantinople.[1]

Under the name of Kahveh Khaneh, this institution was readily adapted to Turkish customs.
Coffee lounges, richly carpeted and provided with
luxurious couches, were the resorts of all manner
of citizens.   To these " schools of the wise " came,
in the first instance, young students and professors ;
persons come up from the country to seek for

[1] The Damascus Coffee House at a later time afforded
one of the most delightful retreats that can be imagined in
the midst of a great city : it was on the river bank, and had
behind it an island planted with trees.   (Pococke's Travels.)
Du Four speaks of three authors who make no mention of
coffee amongst their list of Turkish drinks; the last of these,
Sansovin, wrote in 1563.   According to La Roque, Pichenelli,
their historian, says it was unknown among them until the
year mentioned in the text, i.e. until the reign of Soliman,
whose father, Selim, must have found the custom in Egypt
(see ch. ii. p. 18, of this book).   La Roque says likewise that
Peter Belon (1549) discusses carefully the plants of Egypt
and Arabia without mentioning coffee.

appointments ; lovers of chess or backgammon ; acquaintances whose only thought was to pass away an hour or two in company : each and all found entertainment here for a modest sum—one aspre, which nearly corresponded to a half-penny in our money.

After awhile, when court officials and persons of distinction in the city began to come hither, the suspicion of the authorities, both religious and civil, was aroused.

At Constantinople the religious difficulty speedily appeared ; there were priests and dervishes who accounted it a greater sin to go to a coffee house than to a tavern.   Yet this debate was more easily settled than in Arabia.   As we have already seen (on page 25), a mufti arose with a conscience less tender, or with a less vigorous imagination, than his predecessor, who had declared that the roasted coffee berry must be avoided by the faithful, on the ground that everything resembling " coals " had been by law forbidden.

For a time, indeed, the civil authorities were content to derive a huge income from taxing the popular resorts according to the trade that each was supposed to drive.   But the true despot soon arose, who would not for such considerations allow the growth of what was proving a really political institution.

It happened that there was a war with Candia, and the newsmongers had in the coffee houses taken strange liberties, and, doubtless, had spoken some inconvenient truths. Accordingly, the Grand Vizir determined to strike a sudden and decisive blow. He had " been at the pains to go himself, incognito, to the principal coffee house in the city, where he heard men of gravity and character discoursing seriously concerning the affairs of the empire, and, as a necessary consequence, blaming the ministry." A similar visit of inquiry had been paid to the taverns. Here, indeed, soldiers and others might be found talking loosely, perhaps, and singing or relating their warlike adventures ; but as these poor creatures could do no harm to the Government, the tavern haunts might be tolerated with safety. This led to the paradoxical result that the innocent coffee houses were forbidden, whilst the illicit sale of wine was allowed to continue. But the order does not seem to have extended to many other cities of the Turkish Empire, and even in the suburbs of Constantinople certain coffee houses were allowed to continue open for the sake of the sailors. Moreover, the berry itself was still in request. Its vendors were by no means in despair, and for purposes of trade appeared in the market places, having "large pots with chafing-dishes, and those who have a mind to drink step into any neighbouring shop, where every one is welcome upon such an account."

This prohibition of coffee houses continued long enough to suggest to the English Government a like policy of suppression.

Having now carried our historical sketch down to the time when a knowledge of coffee was brought by travellers from Turkey into Europe, we may add a few interesting particulars concerning the beverage as it came under their notice.

The prohibition of wine had caused the Arabs to search for a substitute; and it was only the discovery of coffee which spoiled the popularity of a certain drink called *cahouat alcatiat* (by some supposed to be tea!) similar in its wakeful effects to coffee, and to this day commonly drunk in parts of Yemen. The Turks likewise had a favourite drink of honey and water, and knew how to make themselves drunk without having recourse to wine.

Sir George Sandys speaks of "sundry sherbets" taken with their water, some of which were made from sugar and lemons, some of violets, and the like. We are also told that they were wont to mix amber with their drink ; the poorer sort con-tented themselves with a something decocted from the juice of raisins.

The decent Turk would have nothing to do with wine, either in the planting or the buying. But temptation was ever at hand, and there will always be some to take a heathenish delight in distressing the conscience of others. Sir George Sandys says :

" Now to that liberty they are growne (the natural Turke excepted) that they will quaffe freely when they come to the house of a Christian: insomuch that I have seene but few go away unled from the Embassadors table. 'Yet,' he con-tinues, 'the feared disorders that might ensue thereof, have been an occasion that divers time all the wine in the City hath bin staved (except in Embassadors houses) and death hath bin made the penalty unto such as presumed to bring any in.'"

The same ineffectual resistance, with bitter repentance to follow, is related by Sir Henry Blunt, in words which make us feel that at any rate the poor Turk had a tender conscience :

" though in that point Mahomet's wise order suffer violence, yet with the better part it prevailes, and makes some drinke with scruple, others with danger; the baser sort, when taken drunke, are often Bastinadoed on the bare feet ; and I have seen some, after a fit of drunkennesse,

lye a whole night crying, and praying to Mahomet for inter-
cession, that I could not sleep neere them; so strong is
conscience even where the foundation is but imaginary."

From other European Christians the Turks got
even less credit in the matter.   Rauwolf[1] says
they " love wine better if their law would allow
it," but when permitted and greedily taken, the
effect was, " as you may easily guess, they become
to be sordid presently, and so hoggish, that they
excel all other nations in it."   Another declares,
on the contrary, that they neglect wine, not in
order that they may conform to the law, but
rather on account of the bad opinion entertained
of what they call the destruction of the memory,
a very plague, and a fatal poison.

Debarred alike from politics and wine, the Turk
sought, and was at one time freely permitted to
find, his solace in new places of entertainment—
diversoria, as they are called by Cotovicus.   The
people flocked thither in endless numbers, and at
almost every hour of the day, with a view to satis-

[1] The first European who has mentioned coffee.   His
"Itinerarium Orientis" (1583) was translated from the
German by Staphorst, and edited by John Ray : see Pt. I.
ch. viii. p. 92.   The last named, a celebrated botanist, incurs
the wrath of Dr. Douglas (see Appendix to *Coffee Tree*)
for believing 'the story "that the Arabians spoil the
Germinative Faculty of the Coffee Fruit" before exportation.

fying an inordinate desire for the drink itself
(*hujus aquæ . . . appetentissimi*), and in the hope
of " entertainment and pastime, making the hours
to slip away merrily in conversation," or, as our
Latin author has it, "*confabulationibus terunt tem-
pus.*" A later traveller, writing, however, before
the time of English coffee houses, compares these
places to taverns, and mentions the custom of employing on the premises " beautiful boyes " as
a special attraction to guests.

"There they sit," he adds, " chatting most of the day and
sippe of a drink called coffee, in little china dishes, as hot
as they can suffer it : blacke as soote and tasting not unlike
it."

Coffee itself was never out of season, for at all
times of the year they took " this drink of a black
colour, which, during the summer is very cooling,
whereas in the winter it mightily heats and warms
the body, yet [wonder to relate !] without changing
the substance and always continuing the same
drink." Thevenot, not at all anticipating the
fervour with which his countrymen would yet
come to regard the matter, remarks, as an onlooker,
that the liquor " smells a little of the burnt, too ;
every one drinks it little by little [' drop by drop
they take it in,' said Cotovicus], for fear of scalding

their mouths," so that one may perceive " a kind of musicke and divertisement by hearing the noise that every one makes in sipping."

The lounging habits of the East, and the desire to escape from the privacy of home, which seems to amount to a passion even in a country so far west as France, tended to make these gatherings universal among the Turks. The Parisian café, half within doors and half in the open air, bears some resemblance to the style of a *cavehane*, this last being " an open shop where you may sit down on the ground or carpet and drink together ; " and " there, upon scaffolds halfe a yard high, covered with mats, they sit crosse-legg'd, after the Turkish manner, many times two or three hundred together, and some poore musicke passing up and downe."

This last description is from Sir Henry, or, as he was then styled, Master Harry Blunt, upon whose mind the impression left was lifelong, and destined to lead to important results. In our next chapter we shall see that the less favourable reports of other travellers alarmed our countrymen, and caused them to fight shy of the drink for a number of years. A knowledge of its existence had reached England from two separate

quarters a short time after the accession of
James I. William Finch, merchant, kept a journal of his voyage to Africa, and at Sierra Leone,
in August, 1607, has the following quaint entry
concerning a custom of the inhabitants with which
he was by no means familiar :

"Tobacco is planted about every man's house, which
seemeth half their food : the boll of their Tobacco pipe is
very large. . . . In the lower end thereof they thrust in a
small hollow cane, a foot and a halfe long, thorow which they
sucke it, both men and women drinking the most part down,
each man carrying in his snap-sack a small purse (called
Taffio) full of Tobacco and his Pipe."

At Socotra, whither he seems to have set out
immediately, he meets with a second surprise.
The people of the country, some of them being
Arabs, appear to be poor, and are beggars in their
poverty ; yet they win the merchant's respect by
giving "faire usage" and by an honest desire to
buy what they can. Moreover, they possess one
luxury, and know how to present this with advantage.

"Their best entertainment is a china dish of Coho, a
blacke bitterish drinke, made of a berry like a Bayberry,
brought from Mecca, supped off hot, good for the head and
stomache."

We may conclude with the black letter original

of Guilelmus Biddulphus, this being the earliest English account of the drink and its customs amongst the Turks which has come down to us at first hand.[1]

---

[1] The quotation on p. 45 is from " Purchas his Pilgrims," who gives it as an extract (ending abruptly) from " Observations of Wm. Finch, Merchant, taken out of his large Journall." Purchas handled his authorities with freedom : " I have thought good to set down such pleasant things as either I found written in their letters or else heard of others who have been in those countries." In his edition of " The Travels of certain Englishmen into Africa, Asia, Syria, &c. Begunne in the yeere of Jubile 1600, and by some of them finished this yeere 1608. The others not yet returned." Purchas omits Biddulph's mention (see black letter ed. of 1609), of what he had seen on the Rhine " this present yeere 1608, July 7." However the passage in question is shown by internal evidence to have been inserted after the traveller's return. That the letter was *written* at the end of 1603 may be concluded from the fact that he had lately heard in Syria (where he had been 'now two yeres fully expired') of the accession of James I., and spoke of the death " not long since " of one Wm. Martin who, according to a marginal note, was killed on September 18th, 1603.

It is accounted a great curtesie amongst them to giue vnto their frends when they come to visit them, a Fin-ion oz Scudella of Coffa, which is moze holesome than toothsome, foz it causeth good concoction, and dziueth away dzowsinesse.

Their most common dzinke is Coffa, which Coffa. is a blacke kind of dzinke made of a kind of Pulse like Pease, called Coaua; which being growend in the mill, and boiled in water, they dzinke it as hot as they can suffer it; which they find to agrée very well with them against their crudities and féeding on hearbs and rawe meates.

Their Coffa houses are moze common than Ale-houses in England; but they vse not so much to sit in the houses as on benches on both sides the stréets néere vnto a Coffa house, euery man with his Fin-ion full, which being smoking hot, they vse to put it to their noses & eares, and then sup it off by leasure, being full of idle and Ale-house talke whiles they are amongst themselues dzinking of it; if there be any news, it is talked of there.

(*Reproduced by Photography.*)

CHAPTER IV.

MEDICAL HISTORY.

"The Drink comforteth the Brain and Heart, and helpeth Digestion."—*Bacon.*
"This drink hath many good physicall properties therein."
—*Parkinson.*

As coffee travelled further towards the west attempts were made to give it a sacred association, which remind us of the old controversy concerning the Koran. For example, a French author named Du Mont wished to have it believed that coffee was the identical red pottage for which Esau sold his birthright, and that the parched grain which Boaz ordered to be given to Ruth was undoubtedly roasted coffee-berries. After this it is but a small thing to adopt the conjecture of "the illustrious Italian traveller," Pietro del Lavalle, that "it would be the Nepenthe that Homer mentions, which Helen drunk there (in Egypt), it being for certain that cahue is brought hither from that country." Once more, a treatise published in England (see page 84) mentions it as a possible objection against coffee, that "the use and the eating of beans were heretofore forbidden by Pythagoras, because that their flowers being spotted with a black colour, did present a melancholy shape, etc., etc."

However, the very absurdity of such opinions prevented their having so great an effect as a certain mistake which may be traced back to the time when coffee was beginning to be known. The fruit and beverage made from it have been called by something like a score of names, most of which are more or less faithful renderings of the Arabic original. The plant itself was called ban, or bon, in Egypt, and the confusion, says Dr. Douglas, was due to the similarity of this last word with one used by two learned Arabians, who flourished as long ago as the tenth century. In the Latin translation of the latter is a quaint discourse upon the various medical properties of the said plant, ending up with the statement : " Bunchum est bonum stomacho." But to Avicenna's question, "Bunchum quid est ?" we must reply that bunchum (or bunkum as one writer spells it) has nothing to do with coffee. Rauwolf and Alpinus, who wrote at the close of the sixteenth century, were wrong in supposing that these early botanists were acquainted with the coffee plant, and in ascribing to them the honour of its earliest mention, which honour was in reality their own.

The fate of this beverage may remind us of the proverb which speaks of being preserved from the indiscretion of friendship, for it never really gained anything by being so solemnly introduced to the public as a medicine. One of the first English authors who mentioned the drink called it " more wholesome than toothsome," and this was its condemnation. The friends of coffee were exaggerating its merits when they called it a powerful medicine, and the enemy made bold to proclaim it as a slow poison : " I think it must be, for I have been drinking it for eighty years and am not dead yet," was the retort of a quick-witted Frenchman.[1] Yet many who would have gladly accepted the

---

[1] Fontenelle, or possibly Voltaire (see " Notes and Queries," 6th Series, iv., 512). The latter, by combining two separate statements, invented a famous saying. Madame de Sevigné never wrote " Racine passera comme le café " to her daughter. What Madame really said was that Racine was writing for Champmeslé, the actress, and not for posterity : again, of coffee she prophesied " s'en dégoûterait comme d'un indigne favori."

" wakeful, innocent drink," shrank back in horror as from a twofold risk.

Amongst its " many good physicall properties," coffee was generally admitted to act as a stimulus to the brain, and perhaps its effect on water-drinkers in the East would be more readily perceived than in our sluggish climate. A magic power to keep its votaries awake through the hours of the night has been already mentioned ; but the writer of our old Arabic manuscript points out that coffee is not unique in this respect, as there are other means by which the same result may be obtained, e.g. " eating little, avoiding all fatigue during the day, taking the noon-day nap, and other practices which are set forth in the book of the Sofis." Nor has the charm always worked in the same manner : Du Four argued that coffee did not interfere with natural sleep, and that in some cases it had been given in order to bring on a peaceful slumber.

A contest that was in some respects a repetition of what took place at Mecca and Cairo is recorded by another Frenchman. However, the public condemnation at Marseilles on February 27, 1679--80 being entirely due to professional jealousy, was not backed up by any similar display of popular fanaticism. In the case before us, we cannot but

admire the adroitness with which the doctors seized
an opportunity for affixing a stigma upon the custom of coffee drinking, whilst they avoided the
full responsibility of what soon proved an utterly
impracticable decision. A youthful applicant for
admission to the College of Physicians was required to draw up and deliver in the Town Hall a
thesis upon the subject. Accordingly, in reply to
the question, " Is the use of coffee hurtful to the
inhabitants of Marseilles ? " the disputant declared
that

"Amongst an infinite number of medicines wherewith the
Arabians have loaded physick, there is none that all nations
have more readily gone into than the drink called coffee;
. . . in this country it has almost abolished the use of wine,
by reason of the excellent qualities that have been ascribed
to it ; though the truth of the matter is that it does not come
up so much as to the dregs of wine, neither in colour, smell,
substance nor qualities."

He then proceeded gravely to explain this widespread and mischievous popularity on the ground
that people in general were taken in by a kind of
punning sophistry : " because the Arabians call it
Bon in their language, and because it comes from
that part of Arabia called the Happy." The
thesis itself, says Dr. Douglas, from whose version
I have been quoting, was no more than a heap of

ill-digested learning, and if it may be judged from the following curious extract we cannot at all wonder that its effect was even less than that produced by the sermons of the Mohammedan preachers. Adopting the scholastic terms, he urges as a certainty

" That coffee is hot and dry, not only from the authority of the authors whom I have mentioned, but also from the chief and most sensible effects of it ; for the adust particles of which it consists are so subtle, and have so great a degree of motion belonging to them, that being mixed with the mass of blood, they carry along with them all the serum into other parts of the body ; from thence they directly attack the brain, where, after having dissolved all the humidity and grosser corpuscles they find there, they keep all the pores of it open, and so hinder the animal spirits, the true causes of sleep, from getting the length of the middle of the brain when these pores come to be shut ; from whence it happens that these adust particles, by the qualities that they are possessed of, do often cause such obstinate watchings, that the nervous juices absolutely necessary for recruiting the spirits come totally to fail, the nerves relax, and a weakness or palsy ensues ; and by the sharpness and dryness of the blood, already quite burnt up, all the parts of the body are drained of their moisture to such a degree as that the whole is reduced to a horrible leanness. All these mischiefs in a special manner befall such as are of a bilious temperament, or melancholy, and whose liver and brain are naturally hot ; in a word, such whose spirits are most subtle, and their blood most burnt up. From all which we cannot help concluding, that the use of coffee is prejudicial to the greater part of the inhabitants of Marseilles."

Whether any of those present ever ventured to

taste again a cup of coffee, and whether terror or
bewilderment was the uppermost feeling in the
minds of the audience, are questions which perhaps
need no reply. It cannot however be doubted
that the orthodox opinion so oddly expressed at
the close of this harangue procured a warm welcome for the candidate amongst the members of
that learned though somewhat prejudiced body,
the College of Physicians at Marseilles.[1]

What Frenchmen dreaded on the ground that
it might produce melancholy, was accepted in this

[1] La Roque says that Thevenot made the use of coffee
general in Marseilles, but was not the first to bring it into
France. This honour he claims for his father, who in 1644
brought coffee and "all the little implements used about it
in Turkey, which were then looked upon as great curiosities
in France." A coffee house was not set up in Marseilles
till 1671. A year later the attempt was made to start a
coffee house in Paris (see page 85), where the beverage had
been in request since the embassy from the Grand Seignior
to Louis in 1669. La Roque relates that in 1695 a thesis
was delivered at Paris publicly condemning coffee. This
dislike on the part of the French is accounted for by Buckle
the historian (quoting Monteil) on the ground that Englishmen, whose politics were then held in detestation, had a
peculiar fondness for the beverage.

The passage in the following paragraph of the text is,
as Mr. John Ashton points out (in his recently published
"Drinks of the World"), not contained in the earliest edition
of Burton's "Anatomy;" it occurs first in the edition of 1632,
published at Oxford.

island as a possible cure for the same, and as an incentive to hilarity. To say that our ancestors suffered more from melancholia than we do in these mournful times would be a rash statement indeed, yet they certainly were at some pains to examine their feelings of this sort: Burton's "Anatomy" proved to them a mine of interest, and so attractive was it to Dr. Johnson, that he spoke of it as the one book that made him rise from his bed in the morning two hours earlier than he otherwise would. In a chapter devoted to the "Cure of Head-Melancholy," Burton makes early mention of coffee, telling how the Turks "find by experience that kind of drink, so used, helpeth digestion and procureth alacrity. Some of them take opium for this purpose." Again, speaking with enthusiasm of the company to be met with in a tavern as the "summum bonum of tradesmen, their felicity, life and soul, their chief comfort, to be merry together," he likens all this to the style of the Turks in their coffee houses.

Travellers had sometimes praised the invigorating effects of coffee, and the more favourable points of their report are summed up in the following passage from Bacon's "Sylva Sylvarum" (written,

though not published, in 1624, i.e. several years
before Burton's description) :

"They have in Turkey a drink called coffee made of a
berry of the same name, as black as soot, and of a strong
scent (but not aromatical), which they take beaten into
powder, in water, as hot as they can drink it ; and they
take it, and sit at it in their coffee houses, which are like
our taverns. The drink comforteth the Brain, and Heart,
and helpeth Digestion."

Yet according to a translation published in
Oxford (see page 84, an Arabic author complains that it sometimes breeds melancholy, causes
headache, "and maketh lean much;" he that
would drink it for liveliness sake and to disperse
slothfulness, "let him use much sweet meates with
it, and oyle of pistacios, and butter. It may be
good against small pox, though to drink it with
milk is an error and such as may bring in danger
of leprosy." It was observed, at a later time, that
any ill effects caused by this drink, unlike those of
tea, etc., cease to operate when it is no longer used.
So, too, Dr. Mosely, suggesting that the original
meaning of the word coffee may be "vigour,"
wishes to see it again in common use as "a cheap
substitute for those enervating teas and beverages
which produce the pernicious habit of dram-
drinking." A somewhat curious account of the
drink originally derived from the Bishop of Berytus

HEADING OF BROADSIDE, 1674.

may be referred to here as showing its importance whenever the water is not fit to be taken by itself. The bishop is on his way to Cochin China by the overland route, he speaks of serious trouble in the desert on this account, and, recording his thanks to the Divine Providence, says,—

"As the water they meet with is commonly naught, petryfied, to correct the indisposition which it causes in the stomach, the Turks take a drink called coffee, which begins to be used by the Europeans. This . . . . sufficiently imitates the effect of wine . . . . has not an agreeable taste but rather bitter, yet it is much used by these people for the good effects they find therein."

A "Granado" discharged against the growing repute of coffee gave a sarcastic account of the "strange, wonderful and miraculous cures" performed thereby, and with similar banter declared "it is for health beyond all cordial drink." However, it seemed no slight gain to those who drank it when they found that by keeping up their spirits they avoided the necessity for taking medicine. Dr. Willis, a learned and highly distinguished physician at Oxford, says that he would sometimes send his patients to the coffee house rather than to the apothecary's shop. An old broadside [1]

[1] Published in 1674, see Illustration and ch. vi., p. 109, "The Coffee Man's Granado discharged upon the Maiden's

lays special stress on the fact that if you but "this
Rare Arabian Cordial Use, then thou may'st all
the Doctors' shops refuse." From the outset this
rhyming advertisement assumes the importance of
an epic poem, and this its air of grandeur is, with
an occasional bathos, carefully sustained throughout :

> When the sweet Poison of the Treacherous Grape
> Had acted on the world a general rape ;
> Drowning our Reason and our souls
> In such deep seas of large o'erflowing bowls,
>
> . . . .
>
> When foggy Ale, leavying up mighty trains
> Of muddy vapours, had besieg'd our Brains,
> Then Heaven in Pity . . . .
> First sent amongst us this All-healing Berry,
>
> . . . .
>
> Coffee arrives, that grave and wholesome Liquor,
> That heals the stomach, makes the genius quicker,
> Relieves the memory, revives the sad,
> And cheers the Spirits, without making mad ;
> And soon despatcheth . . . .
> Whatso'ere with Nature leavyeth Warrs ;
> It helps Digestion, want of Appetite,
> And quickly sets Consumptive bodies right ;
>
> . . . .

Complaint against Coffee " was fulminated in 1663. See the
Bibliography for a chronological list of pamphlets and broadsides quoted in the following chapters of this book according
to their references to the social side of our subject or to
politics.

Hush then, dull Quacks, your Mountebanking cease,
COFFEE'S a speedier cure for each Disease,
How great its virtues are we hence may think,
The world's third part makes it 'their Common Drink.

This Poem falters somewhat towards the close, and perhaps it was not judicious in so pretentious a composition to descend to "ruby noses, or blear'd eyes:" we must not be too critical about the exact balance and rhyming of the couplets; otherwise the poet is himself again in the last few lines of his final exhortation :

In Brief, all you who Health's rich treasures prize,
And court not ruby noses, or blear'd eyes,
But own sobriety to be your drift,
And love at once good Company and Thrift;
To Wine no more make Wit and coyn a trophy,
But come each Night and Froliq'ue here in Coffee.

It may be something of a relief to pass from these high imaginings to the commonplace of prose. We come next to the book in which Justice Rumsey described by a Latin title, viz. Organon Salutis, his newly-invented cleansing instrument.[1]

[1] The first edition is advertised as follows in the *Mercurius Politicus* for Thursday, June 11th, to June 18th, 1657: " Organon Salutis, An Instrument to cleanse the Stomach, as also divers new Experiments of the virtue of

Of the unpleasant invention little need be said, except that it was made of whalebone and was much in repute amongst foreigners. Nor can we suppose that Rumsey's "Electuary of Cophy" would obtain much favour amongst Englishmen, admirably contrived as it was for an auxiliary to the machine itself. The prescription is as follows:

> " Take equal quantity of Butter and Sallet-oil, melt them well together, but not boyle them : then stir them well that they may incorporate together : then melt therewith three times as much Honey, and stir it well together : then add thereunto powder of Turkish Cophie, to make it a thick Electuary."

Another concoction of the worthy judge, for so he was called, included Oatmeal, powder of Cophie, a pint of Ale or any wine, ginger, honey, or sugar to please the taste ; to these ingredients butter might be added and any cordial powder or pleasant spice. One was to put it into a flannel bag and "so keep it at pleasure like starch." Such was the elaborate preparation considered necessary in those days, if the unpleasant taste of coffee was to pass unnoticed. When it is added that this kind

Tobacco and Coffee ; by W. Rumsey, of Gray s Inn, Esquire. Both sold by D. Pakeman at the Rainbow, near the Inner Temple Gate." For Pakeman, a law bookseller, and for Sir Henry Blunt at the Rainbow, see ch. v. p. 92, &c.

of medicine, which he significantly calls "Wash-brew," was used by the common people of Wales, we can only suppose that the judge himself had a very widespread jurisdiction in those parts. Yet he did not despair of its reception in England, for a hope is expressed that in this form the Turk's physic would ultimately prove "as common to be sold as the new cophy-houses sell boiled cophy." The object in view was to render this nauseous drug "less loathsome and troublesome." In a friendly letter to the author from Sir Henry Blunt, we are told that whilst

"Coffee and Tobacco have not the advantage of any pleasing taste wherewith to tempt and debauch our palat, as Wine and other such pernicious things have; for at first Tobacco is most horrid, and Cophie insipid,"

yet they are, in foreign parts, more universally adopted than bread itself. It should be noticed that this unflattering description comes from the pen of one who was ever a staunch upholder of coffee drinking, and is at least equalled by the quaint advocacy of the pamphlet (of 1675) which says,—

"For its taste, it is a pitiful childish humour always to indulge our palates."

Sir Henry's letter fully supports an uncommon

repute for extravagant tales. He speaks of coffee as being among the Turks an acknowledged remedy for the effects of "ill diet or moist lodging ;" furthermore, when one of them is sick he fasts, takes coffee, and, if that is of no avail, " makes his will and thinks of no other Physick." Yet even this Traveller's Tale does not come up to what might be termed an allegory, its connexion with the foregoing prescriptions being sufficiently apparent, were it not introduced by the judge as "a strange history which I know to be true." It is here given in his own words, with full apologies to the reader :

" An old souldier, and a Commander in Queen Elizabeth's time, in the Low Countries, was drinking of healths amongst his companions, and at every health he did drink a pistol bullet, to the number of eighteen ; which continued in his stomach for neer the space of two years, with much pain and grief. He acquainted a physician with his case, who did hang the souldier by the heels, by a beam in the chamber ; and then all the bullets dropped out of his mouth again ; . . . . This soldier is yet living, and in good health, and about fourscore and ten years of age."

It would not be easy to exhaust the list of virtues ascribed to this beverage. The occult science of tossing coffee grounds was at one time in vogue. However, this art of Divination, by which might be procured, with a single cast of the cup, "a picture of all one's life to come," was the ingenious product of a later age. Not less wonderful and of more practical importance was the prevalent opinion that coffee possessed a sort of magic power for the cure of drunkenness. Perhaps the earliest mention of this curious notion is to be found in the "Character of a Coffee House" for 1665, where a man is described as sitting "now demure and sober" who was "within this hour quite drunk;" and the rhymster adds, "he comes here frequently, for 'tis his daily malady." [1]   Upon

---

[1] "There is nothing more effectual than this reviving drink," says the pamphleteer of 1675, "to restore their senses that have brutified themselves by immoderate tippling heady liquors." More grudgingly the pamphlet of 1672 admits the same : "but to cure Drunkards it has got great fame." Du Four, in 1683, relates how on one occasion a friend of his regained both sight and cunning, after he had succumbed to the influence of wine so far as to be unable to distinguish between the cards at a game of piquet. Gonzales ("Pinkerton's Voyages," vol. II. p. 92) says at a later time, "some when they have taken a handsome dose run to the coffee house at midnight for a dish of coffee to set them right." Coffee has been praised by one writer as a deodorizer : another (Bradley) in his Treatise concerning its use with regard to the Plague and other infectious Disorders, says that if its qualities had been fully known in 1665, "Dr. Hodges and other learned men of that time would have recommended it." In Gideon Harvey's "Advice

the same topic we have the following anagram which, as the author of the "Rebellious Antidote" himself admits, was not composed without some forcing of his muse :

Come, Frantick Fools, leave off your Drunken fits,
Obsequious be and I'll recall your Wits,
From perfect Madness to a modest Strain,
For Farthings four I'll fetch you back again,
Enable all your mene with tricks of State,
Enter and sip and then attend your Fate ;
Come Drunk or Sober, for a gentle Fee,
Come n'er so Mad, I'll your Physician be.

When we come to consider the Temperance aspect of our subject it will appear that this invitation was accepted literally, and that the characters who flocked hither from the tavern just before the nine o'clock closing hour were not always such as to improve the reputation of the institution.

That the coffee men were willing to make the most of their supposed power over inebriates is clear from an advertisement which, after discoursing in the usual manner upon "The Nature, quality and most Excellent Vertues of Coffee," adds pertinent advice to those who need it : " art thou

against the Plague," published in 1665, we find that " Coffee is commended against the contagion."

surfeited with gluttony or Drunkenness, then let this be thy common Drink." In our next chapter we shall have more to say concerning the origin and date of these early commendations. The following specimen is here inserted that the reader may see how completely the true merits of the beverage were lost to sight by those who urged its more fantastic claims :

The Vertue of the COFFEE Drink. First publiquely made and sold in England by Pasqua Rosee.

The Grain or Berry called Coffee, groweth upon little Trees, only in the Deserts of Arabia. It is brought from thence, and drunk generally throughout all the Grand Seignior's Dominions. It is a simple innocent thing, composed into a drink by being dryed in an oven, and ground to powder, and boiled up with spring water, and about half a pint of it to be drunk, fasting an hour before, and not eating an hour after, and to be taken as hot as possibly can be endured; the which will never fetch the skin off the mouth, or raise any blisters, by reason of that Heat.

The Turks' drink at meals and other times is usually water, and their dyet consists much of fruit; the crudities whereof are very much corrected by this drink.

The quality of this drink is cold and dry; and though it be a Dryer, yet it neither heats, nor inflames more than *hot Posset.* . . . . it is very good to help digestion ; and therefore of great use to be taken about three or four a clock afternoon, as well as in the morning. It much quickens the spirits, and makes the heart lightsome; it is good against sore eys, and the better if you hold your head over it and take in the steem that way.

Further, it is good for the headache, for con-

sumptions, coughs, king's evil, dropsy and gout.
Besides curing almost every disease to which mankind is heir, we learn that the beverage is suited to
old age and to tender infancy.   It will exert its
power in cases of melancholy, and prevents drowsiness if one has occasion to watch.   It is not to be
regarded as too powerful a medicine, and according
to the last paragraph of this early puff the most
wonderful effect of coffee is wrought upon the
outward appearance of a man: for in Turkey,
where it is generally drunk, "their skins are ex-
ceeding white and clear."

In the cautious estimate of this drug which Dr.
Willis has given in his "Pharmaceutice Rationalis,"
we have an early attempt to discriminate and to
do justice to both sides of the question.   Coffee is
still regarded as a risky beverage.   Its votaries
must in some cases be prepared to encounter
languor and even paralysis; it may attack the
heart and affect the limbs with trembling.   On the
other hand it may, if judiciously used, prove a
marvellous benefit; "being daily drunk it wonder-
fully clears and enlightens each part of the Soul,
and disperses all the clouds of every Function." [1]

----

[1] See vii. cap. 3, "assidue haustus utramque animae
partem mire clarificat, et illustrat, atque functionum

Dr. Willis, one of the earliest members of the Royal Society, was a distinguished pioneer, and his encouragement aided the progress which we shall presently have to report as taking place at Oxford. We might indeed conjure by a far more enduring name. One who spoke of William Harvey from recollection, tells how he and his brother were accustomed to patronize the beverage before coffee houses became a fashion in London.[1]

quarumcunque nebulas omnes dispellit .... verum è contra, qui graciles, et temperamenti biliosi aut melancholici .... à potu isto prorsus abstinere debent." The translation in the text is from Sir T. Pope Blount's Natural History. Dr. Willis was known for his clever "Anatomy of the Brain." His bold theories startled contemporaries, and Portal. is said to have called him "one of the greatest geniuses that ever lived." In the year (1674) that he published his " Pharm. Rationalis," a women's petition (quoted by D'Israeli and others) was got up against the drink. Besides the more serious complaint that the whole race was in danger of extinction, it was urged that "on a domestic message a husband would stop by the way to drink a couple of cups of coffee." This called forth at once a "Man's answer to the Women's petition."

[1] Harvey, born in 1578, and educated at Gonville and Caius Coll., lived to about the age of eighty. "I remember," says Aubrey, "he was wont to drinke coffee; which he and his brother Eliab did, before coffee houses were in fashion in London" ("Lives of Eminent Men," vol. II., pt. 2, pp. 384, 5.) Houghton in 1701 speaks of "the famous inventor of the Circulation of the Blood, Dr. Harvey, who some say did frequently use it."

It is, however, almost time to conclude with the admission that coffee is, after all, "a simple, innocent thing," and that if any beyond social virtues are to be found therein these are " political rather than medical." We may not wholly reject the evidence of Du Four and of many others who have borne witness to the use of coffee in preventing or alleviating gout, and to its potency in certain cases of nervous disorder. Yet it is evident that the progress of medical science has thrown into the shade "the Turk's physick," replacing this, together with many another homely remedy, by drugs that are more certain in their operation as well as more powerful. The tone of exaggeration was gradually modified, as we may see from Dr. Duncan's "Wholesome advice against the abuse of hot liquors," published at the beginning of the eighteenth century. In his somewhat lengthy treatise (280 pages being almost exclusively devoted to coffee), the doctor inveighs against consulting our depraved taste in this matter, lest coffee, which relishes of a burnt sulphur, should lose its reputation and be banished "from the catalogue of those good things which tend to preserve health." On the other hand, persons in health have no more reason to drink coffee continually than to take a dose of physic daily. Nor is the doctor wholly free from the trammels of the ancients when he argues thus : Suppose coffee, chocolate and tea to be either cold or hot, which of them you please, it cannot but be destructive to such as are cold or hot already. Yet he grows weary of perpetual mystery, and honestly exclaims, " Coffee does not burn ; " so they say, but that does not prevent the scalding effects of the water in which it is mixed ! Again, coffee no more deserves the name of panacea than that of poison. Surely physicians are human and liable after all to mix with prescriptions a grain of their own inclination. When M. le Closure, a noted doctor of Perigueux, ordered all his patients to be physicked with coffee, was it not because he loved it mightily himself ? Likewise, its wholesale prohibition by another member of the profession may have been due to his violent and personal dislike of the beverage.

Similarly, George Cheyne is made to remark that it is as dangerous, "at least in thin and dry habits, to dabble in it two or three times every day, as it would be for such to drink nothing but scalding lime water." Whilst however some doctors had gone out of their way to condemn this "kind of burnt horse-bean," and others had as extravagantly commended, he would go to neither extreme. Whereas to its influence had been attributed the frequency of scurvy, vapours, low-spiritedness, and nervous distempers, he believed that the cause was not adequate to the effect. In the earlier (1726) and more trustworthy Latin edition of his work, Cheyne's nearest approach to neutrality is concisely expressed: " ego nec magnae laudis nec maximi vituperii rem esse existimo."

CHAPTER V.

EARLIEST COFFEE HOUSES UNDER THE COMMONWEALTH.

> So great a universitie
> I think there ne'er was any,
> In which you may a scholar be,
> For spending of a penny.

THE exact date when coffee was first drunk in England is uncertain, though Nathaniel Conopius, a Cretan, who lived for some years at Oxford and was expelled during the troubles of 1648, was known to have made coffee for his own use while he continued at Balliol College.[1]

[1] Sent thither by Laud. He was afterwards made Bishop of Smyrna. Wood says "he was expelled the university by the barbarians, I mean the Parliamentarian Visitors . . . . while he continued in Balliol College he made the drink for his own use called coffee, and usually drank it every morning, being the first, as the antients of that house have informed me, that was ever drank in Oxon." As Montagu Burrows points out in his " Register of the Visitors of the University of Oxford," Wood's after-productions (e.g. the " Annals " and " Athenæ Oxon.") are coloured by opinions of the later Caroline period. Mr. Burrows does justice to the

The year 1650 was not one of cheerful memory amongst the scholars of the University. They had already been made to suffer for their loyalty to the fallen cause of monarchy, and were now compelled to forbear all excess and vanity in powdering their hair and wearing knots of ribands, whether in hat or clothes, to give up the keeping of hounds and horses, which had lately become a common practice, and to doff their sportsman-like costume, e.g. "spurs, and boot-hose tops." These vexatious orders were issued by a Parliamentary Board of Visitors, concerning whose doings, registered with minutest accuracy by Anthony à Wood, we shall have more to say presently. Amongst other quaint particulars, Wood has jotted down in his "Annals" the fact, that one Jacob, a Jew, opened at the Angel, in the parish of St. Peter in the

work of the Parliamentary Board in his "History of All Souls' College." Mr. Andrew Clark's "Life and Times of Anthony Wood," is the latest and best edition of the Antiquary's labours. Since we say Daniel *De* Foe, why not allow the signature, as it was always written in later years, Anthony à Wood?

Evelyn (Diary, vol. I., page 10—date, May 10, 1637) makes mention of the Cretan : "There came in my time to the College one Nathaniel Conopios, out of Greece. . . . He was the first I ever saw drink coffee ; which custom came not into England till thirty years after" [!].

East, what was not merely the earliest English coffee house, but the first, by a single year, which is known for a certainty to have existed in Christendom. Accordingly, about the year 1650, coffee and chocolate began to be frequently taken, and at this place the former " was, by some who delighted in noveltie, drank."

Four years later we find that Cirques Jobson, a Jew and a Jacobite (i.e. belonging to a sect of monophysite Christians), born near Mount Libanus, also described as an " outlander," was selling coffee and chocolate " in an house between Edmund Hall and Queen College Corner." Wood gives us most of these particulars a second time, and says in his Diary that this was " at or neare the Angel within the East Gate of Oxon." There was probably some connection between these two, the former coffee man may have already handed over the business and retired to London where, in Southampton Buildings, Holborn, he was to be found at a later time carrying on the same trade. Doubtless the Jews, who by Cromwell's generous policy were allowed to settle once more in England, would bring with them from abroad the berry so highly praised by their master the Turk.

We come next to consider Wood's account of

the society of young students who, in the year
1655, encouraged an apothecary named Arthur
Tillyard to sell "coffey publickly in his House
against all Soules College." This Tillyard, who
could in so remarkable a manner unite the dangerous callings of "Apothecary and Royallist"
("Apothecary and Great Royallist," says Wood
in the "Life"), must himself have been somewhat
of a character. Though several of his visitors were
as heartily devoted to the same cause, there is no
reason to accept the suggestion that they were a
club or clique of men who, not daring to drink the
health of the young Charles in any ordinary way,
thought to do so with less risk in what was not
yet regarded as a political beverage. It may be
said, that in those days of gloomy strictness coffee
being a luxury would meet with its best chance of
protection under the shadow of a college which
offered strenuous opposition to the reforming zeal
of the Puritans. Yet it is curious that of the
Fellows who were appointed during the time
that the Parliamentary Visitors held office, four
were members of the club in question. Two
of these, viz. Thomas Millington [1] and Peter

[1] Physician, a member of Peter Sthael's class, Professor
of Natural Philosophy, being successor to Dr. Willis. He

Pett[1] were not without renown in after days : a third, who did not rise to eminence, was William Bull.[2] The fourth had recently, with permission of the Visitors, been appointed to his fellowship by a free college election. For eight years of his life the great architect, Sir Christopher Wren—for it was no less than he—was connected with All Souls' College. He was already showing such abundant proof of genius as called forth the enthusiasm of his friends.[3]

was knighted and became physician in ordinary to King William III.

[1] One of the earliest members of the Royal Society, Advocate-General to Charles II., and knighted.

[2] Gentleman Commoner of Trinity College ; became Fellow of All Souls' in 1654. Like Wood he had a taste for music, and this perhaps brought them together. They were companions in a mad frolic which is related with some disgust by Wood himself. Bull was the senior man, and examined his friend for the M.A. degree. From the recently published "Alumni Oxon." we learn that Bull took the degree of B.Med. in 1658 : he died three years later, aged thirty-eight.

[3] Evelyn in his Diary (July 11, 1654), speaks of " being taken up at All Souls', where we had music, voices and theorbos, performed by some ingenious scholars. After dinner I visited that miracle of a youth, Mr. Christopher Wren, nephew to the Bishop of Ely." Two days later Evelyn mentions the same " prodigious young scholar " as having a share in the collection of curios made by " that most obliging and universally curious Dr. Wilkins at Wadham College." Sprat and C. R. Weld speak of this man as belonging to

Three of the number, who were more or less out-
siders, also deserve notice. Matthew and Thomas
Wren, sons of the Bishop of Ely,[1] were staying for a
time in Oxford and joined the company; and last,
but not least, John Lamphire, the physician, lately
ejected from New College, but afterwards restored
to his fellowship. Lamphire is described by Wood
as being "a good, generous and fatherly man, of
a public spirit, and free from pharisaical leven."
He seems indeed to have been of an amiable disposition; knowing full well how to suffer in real

a scientific club, which met as early as 1645 at the Bull's
Head Tavern, Cheapside. Returning to Oxford he took
an active part in the "experimentalle philosophicalle
clubbe, which began 1649, and was incunabile of Royall
Society."

[1] This learned but unfortunate prelate was for eighteen
years confined to the Tower on account of his Royalist
principles, which allowed of no compromise. Evelyn speaks
of Matt. Wren as "that most ingenious gentleman." He
was one of the earliest members of the Royal Society. He
was an active partisan on the Royalist side, and replied to
the arguments of James Harrington by writing "Monarchy
Asserted," etc. He left Cambridge University for Oxford
on account of his father's troubles. Thomas Wren
was also a sojourner at Oxford, and a member of the
Musical Society, in which Wood took an interest. The
Restoration brought him promotion, and in the year 1660
he was, together with John Lamphire, made a Doctor
of Physic. At a later time he became Archdeacon of
Ely.

life, he could also play his humorous part in a merry society, and this worthy man was " sometimes the natural Droll of the company."

When we contrast Wood's evident respect for some of these men with his disdainful treatment of the club as a whole, it becomes fairly evident that they were not a Royalist Society. In one passage he speaks of them as men who esteemed themselves either virtuosi or wits ; and again, at a later date, he says that, " about 1655, a club was erected at Tillyard's, where many pretended wits would meet and deride at others." It is safe to conjecture that the society banished from their midst all serious discussion of political topics, and Wood's dislike is easily explained when we remember that he had little or no taste for the scientific pursuits to which they inclined by way of substitute.

Though the coffee house did not become immediately popular through its introduction at Oxford, it is interesting to see that this institution, and another of which it was a sort of popular edition, met with their first encouragement at the university. The connexion between the earliest coffee club and the small group of students who formed the nucleus of the Royal Society is alike curious

and intricate.   Indeed, at the outset, the distinction between them is so slight that they might
almost be regarded as identical.   They both
originated in the desire to escape from an atmosphere of political strife.   They had some of their
most prominent members in common.   Here were
to be found the same men in varied humours, and
the only difference was due to the fact that even
the gravest philosophers will at some time show a
disposition to unbend—nemo semper sapiens.
Tillyard's coffee club continued until the Restoration, and then Christopher Wren, with his companions, attended a science club or class under the
chemist's hospitable roof.   As to whether or not
coffee was still a part of the entertainment, Wood
does not inform us, and this must be left to the
imagination.[1]

[7] Christopher Wren, says Wood, was a member of the
club or class held by Peter Sthael of Strasburg : " After he
(Sthael) had taken in another class of six there, he translated himself to the house of Arthur Tylliard, an apothecary,
the next door to that of John Cross (saving one, which is a
taverne), where he continued teaching till the latter end of
1662." Sthael was afterwards operator to the Royal
Society. The following confession by Wood shows his own
connection with the matter : " May 30, the Chemical Club
concluded, and A. W. paid Mr. Sthael 30 shill., ... A.
W. got some knowledge and experience; but his mind still
hung after antiquities and musick." With Tillyard him-

The parallel between these two societies may be traced to some extent in their after history. Both movements spread to the capital whilst they continued to flourish at Oxford. The London members of the Royal Society did not relinquish their old tastes, and, as we shall presently see, they sought relaxation from more serious occupations by meeting for friendly and informal discussion at the " Grecian " Coffee House.

Before concluding this account of the coffee houses at Oxford it will be convenient to notice a still bolder comparison which has been employed by enthusiastic admirers. John Houghton, a Cambridge professor, declares that a man might pick up more useful knowledge at these places than he could by application to his books for a whole month, and, in the name of a former member of the Royal Society, ventures to compare these popular resorts with the University itself. That worthy, who was a man of learning, " and had a very good esteem for the universities and they for him," was wont to express the opinion " that coffee houses had improved useful knowledge, as much as they [the universities] have, and spake in

self Wood was evidently acquainted, and has given his pedigree at length.

no way of slight to them neither. They are both best, but I must confess, that he who has been well educated in the schools, is the fittest man to make good use of coffee houses . . ."

Perhaps the one point in which the coffee house system really resembled that of the universities was its power of combining almost endless variety with a certain amount of order. However that may be, the idea of humorously comparing the two was older than Houghton's time, for as the quaint rhyme of 1667 has it :

> So great a universitie
> I think there ne'er was any,
> In which you may a scholar be,
> For spending of a penny.

One is obliged to admit that in Oxford and Cambridge the coffee house was often regarded as a mere parasite upon the tree of knowledge. Wood (in 1661) complains bitterly that scholarly topics have ceased, so that " nothing but news and the affaires of Christendome is discoursed off and that also generally at coffee houses." Some sixteen years later he has the following catechism upon this subject :

" Why doth solid and serious learning decline, and few or none follow it now in the university ? Answer : Because of coffee houses, where they spend all their time; and in entertainments . . . . in common chambers whole afternoons and thence to the coffee house." [1]

Wood's annoyance was doubtless increased by the fact that the Puritans had begun to assemble in a " coffee-academy instituted by Apollo for the advance of Gazett Philosophy by Mercury's, Diurnals, etc.," and there ventured to attack a distinguished writer of the opposite party.[2]

[1] In 1674 Wood makes a similar complaint. In 1677 he records an Order by the Vice-Chancellor, commanding the coffee sellers not to open after evening prayers on Sundays, "nor to permit people to drink it in their houses. . . . This was looked upon as a peak against the Masters: but at 5 of the clock they flocked the more." In 1680 a Puritan mayor forbad it altogether on Sundays.

[2] See "The Censure of the Rota on Mr. Driden's Conquest of Granada "[Oxford, 1673], which called forth amongst other replies one entitled " Mr. Dreyden Vindicated," where a critic is compared to "a country justice in a coffee house, that brings in Henry VIII.'s statutes, or Dalton, upon all occasions to show his reading." In " A description of the Academy of Athenian Virtuosi" (by R. Leigh, not the well-known comedian, see Scott's Dryden, sec. iii. p. 134), four reasons are given to show why a coffee house, rather than a tavern, should be the place of meeting; (1) to hinder expences; (2) to vindicate the sober inclination of the persons; (3) to assist the memory by coffee; (4) because persons of all qualities from all parts resorted to such places. One of these pamphlets, taking Dryden's part, was published at Cambridge, and inveighs against the " gloomy sullen censure of the Rota's."

Similarly, a fierce tirade against the institution as it existed at Cambridge, comes from the pen of a determined advocate of the Stuart Government. Sir Roger North praises the conduct of his relative, Dr. John North, on the ground that he punctually obeyed all Regulations of the College, even to the matter of dining regularly in Hall, except, indeed, "upon a fish day only, being told it was for his health." Nor did he, after the manner which became so general at a later period, waste his time in frivolous entertainment :—

"Whilst he was at Jesus College, coffee was not of such common use as afterwards, and coffee-houses but young. At that Time, and long after, there was but one, kept by one Kirk. The Trade of News also was scarce set up; for they had only the public Gazette, till Kirk got a written news letter circulated by one Muddiman. But now the case is much altered; for it is become a Custom, after Chapel, to repair to one or other of the Coffee Houses (for there are diverse), where Hours are spent in talking, and less profitable reading of News Papers, of which swarms are continually supplied from London. And the Scholars are so Greedy after News (which is none of their business) that they neglect all for it . . . a vast Loss of Time grown out of a pure Novelty, for who can apply close to a subject with his Head full of the Din of a Coffee House? I cannot but think that since coffee, with most, is become a Morning Refreshment, the Order which I once knew established at Lambeth House, or somewhat like it, might be introduced into the Colleges; which was for the Chaplains and Gentlemen officers to meet every morning in a sort of Still-House where a good Woman provided them their Liquors as they liked best; and this they called their Coffee-House." [1]

At a later time an Oxford Professor satirizes the ignorance of his University by a mock exaltation of the institution which may be said to have dimly foreshadowed the glories of the "Union." He says that besides the libraries of Radcliffe and Bodley there have been many "founded in our coffee-houses, for the benefit of such of the Academics as have neglected or lost their Latin and Greek. In these useful repositories *grown gentlemen* are accommodated with the Cyclopædia. . . . The Reviews form the complete Critic, without consulting the dry rules of

---

[1] For a knowledge of the following particulars concerning the college life of Dr. John North, I am indebted to the kindness of the Master of Jesus College. Dr. John North (Master of Trinity College; born 1645, died 1683) was admitted as a Fellow Commoner in February, 1660. He took his degree in 1664, and in the same year obtained a Fellowship which he held continuously until 1671. It was during the earlier part of the Doctor's time at Jesus College that Muddiman was in the Government employ (pp. 141, 142 *Note*). See Appendix for a Cambridge coffee token and for further particulars as to the years 1664 and 1675.

The librarian of Lambeth Palace Library kindly informs me that he has not been able to find, after some time spent in searching, any further trace of "the Order" to which North refers.

Aristotle." Furthermore, "As there are books suited to every taste, so there are Liquors adapted to every species of reading," in so much that "learning remains no longer a *dry* pursuit."[1]

Returning to the earlier period we find that descriptions of the novelty were put forth from time to time at Oxford. In 1659 the learned Edw. Pococke published a short tract, of which the title, "Nature of the Drink Cauhi or Coffee," and the fact that it was a mere translation of the words of an Arab physician, show how little was as yet known in England about this subject. Another pamphlet printed in London (in the year 1685), but dedicated to the Warden of Merton College, points to a further stage of knowledge, though as a translation it is something worse than second-hand. It professes to contain "a curious discourse of coffee . . . not long composed by a very learned physician of Germany [? Strauss] who would be nameless." The translator arouses our interest when he says that there are at Paris many shops selling coffee with a commendation or advertisement which closely resembles the one put forth in

---

[1] "A Companion to the Guide, and Guide to the Companion," by Tom Warton (b. 1728), Professor of Poetry; also quoted by C. W. Boase in his account of Oxford.

English by Pasqua Rosee. This foreigner's bill has been already quoted in Chapter IV., and we now come to consider his adventures when setting up in 1652, the first London coffee house. As regards the French edition, its date can be traced back to the end of 1670, this being rather more than one year before the time when Pascal the Armenian is supposed to have opened the earliest Parisian café.[1]

[1] The English is merely taken from Du Four's compilation ("De l' Usage du Caphé ;" licensed Dec. 17, 1670 ; published 1671). It is really Du Four who tells how coffee was known in several countries of Europe, adding : " Et presentement à Paris, il y a plusieurs Boutiques où l'on vend publiquement le caffé avec l'Eloge suivant. Les tres excellentes vertus de la Meure [i.e. mûre] appellée *coffé* [N.B. This spelling does not *necessarily* imply an English origin]. Coffé est une Meure, qui croist dans les Deserts d'Arabie seulement, d'où elle est transportée dans toutes les dominations du Grand Seigneur, qui estant beuë desseiche toutes humeurs froides et humides, &c., &c." Du Four, at the commencement of this same paragraph, quotes from the "Description of Coffee " published at Oxford in 1659, and Douglas, perhaps in view of this passage, holds Du Four responsible for fixing the date of the French advertisement as early as 1658 (C. T. ii. p. 36). Thus the continued process of translation and reproduction has led to some confusion.

Two similar bills belonging to "the Rainbowe in Fleet Street, between the two Temple Gates," are preserved in the British Museum. Mention of another will be found with Pasqua's in Chapter IV. These printed advertisements were very common, and Wood possessed two which he has marked with the date December, 1660. The former con-

There is no need to conclude that Pascal and Pasqua were identical, though the former, upon the failure of his attempt, fled to England; and the latter, with a still harder fate, found it prudent to retire from the scene of his well-earned success.

The story of Pasqua Rosee is like that of many another who has pointed out the way to fame and fortune without himself being able to reach the goal. This man, a native of Ragusa, was the servant of a merchant named Edwards, who had grown accustomed to the use of coffee at Smyrna, and came together with his master to Leghorn, where they found its use established and the coffee-house an institution.[1] Upon his return to England,

tains a slip with the localization to Oxford entered in writing as follows: "By James Gough at Mr. Surye's the taylor by Queen's Coll. corner Oxon." The latter gives "The virtues of Chocolate (East India drink); the properties of Cavee (Egipt drink)," and states that "these drinks are to be sold at M. [?] Sury's neare East Gate." See "Life and Times of Anthony Wood, by Andrew Clark, M.A.," vol. i. 1891; also compare Wood's description of the place where Cirques Jobson sold coffee and chocolate.

[1] See Appendix B. Coffee had been known in Italy for many years. Lavallè writes of it from Constantinople in 1615: "When I return I will bring some of it with me, and will impart the knowledge of this simple to the Italians, which perhaps at present is altogether unknown to them." Douglas (ii. p. 26) says, on the authority of Veslingius, that

which was reached in 1652, the friends of Mr. Edwards, and in particular an elderly gentleman of the name of Hodges, app ar to have welcomed him with great cordiality. They paid him frequent visits, the special cause of attraction being a new kind of black liquor which the Greek servant was in the habit of preparing for his master every morning; indeed, Mr. Edwards encouraged his friends by a brave example, for he was wont to drink it twice or thrice a day, and two or three dishes at a time. After awhile the merchant began to weary of keeping open house, since he found that this unlooked-for popularity was depriving him of a large part of every day. Accordingly in the same year his servant was instructed to set up for himself a coffee-house to which all might resort without having any further excuse for troubling Mr. Edwards.

The public being informed that coffee was "Made and sold in St. Michael's Alley in Cornhill, by Pasqua Rósee, at the signe of his own Head," accepted the invitation in such numbers that suc-

coffee was probably sold in Italy before 1638, though only as a medicine, "the first step it made from the cabinets of the curious, as an exotick seed, having been into the apothecaries' shops as a drug."

cess appeared certain.   However, his troubles soon
began.   Jealousy had been aroused : the ale-house
keepers took alarm at an innovation which was
threatening already to do them an injury.   Stirred
by a common feeling of danger, they resolved upon
united action, and drew up a petition to the Lord
Mayor, pointing out that the stranger, being in
the business sense of the term " no freeman," had
not a right to carry on this trade.   The timely aid
of his old friends saved Pasqua for once from the
dangers that threatened.   Alderman Hodges, who
in the meantime had given his daughter in marriage
to Mr. Edwards, arranged to do after the manner
of his son-in-law ; he dispensed with the services
of his coachman and sent him forthwith into the
business.   This fellow, named Bowman, was soon
qualified as a freeman, and joined Pasqua in the
coffee trade at St. Michael's Alley ; but the cause
which united their masters does not seem to have
led to a friendship between the servants, for
Bowman, it may be surmised, had already in his
mind another and a different kind of partnership.
After some time they separated, and Bowman set
up a tent or shade in St. Michael's Churchyard,
just opposite to Pasqua, who remained at the same
place of business.   At this juncture a zealous

partisan addressed a copy of verses, "To Pasqua Rosee, at the Sign of his own Head and half his Body, in St. Michael's Alley, next the first Coffee-Tent in London." These lines begin with an odd conceit, the reference being to a supposed drying power of coffee :—

> " Were not the fountain of my Tears
>   Each day exhausted by the steam
> Of your Coffee, no doubt appears
>   But they would swell to such a stream
> As could admit of no restriction,'
> To see, poor Pasqua, thy Affliction.
>
> What ! Pasqua, you at first did broach
>   This Nectar for the publick Good,
> Must you call Kitt down from the Coach
>   To drive a Trade he understood
> No more than you did then your creed,
> Or he doth now to write or read ? "

Pasqua's change in religion ; his attempt (likewise of doubtful merit) to initiate Bowman into the tricks of the trade ; his trouble in making "Kitt" presentable ; and on the other hand the coachman's ignorance, envy, and base ingratitude having been harped upon each in turn, the troubled lines proceed :—

> " Pull Courage, Pasqua, fear no Harms
>   From the besieging Foe ;

> Make good your Ground, stand to your Arms,
>   Hold out this summer, and then tho'
> He'll storm, he ll not prevail—your Face[1]
> Shall give the Coffee Pot the chace."

Yet even the delicate compliments and prophetic utterance of the poet who modestly signs himself "Adrianus del Tasso" could not save "poor Pasqua" from his fate, and he disappeared, possibly to seek a happier fortune elsewhere : it is indeed reported that he ran away in consequence of some misdemeanour, but this may be only the malice of an enemy, and it is enough to remember that the stranger was never really competent to carry on the trade without the help of another.[1]   Not having any longer a rival, the

---

[1] Pasqua's sign, whilst Kitt's (or Bowman's) was perhaps the Coffee-Pot.

[2] The identity of Pasqua seems to have been merged in that of his former pupil, and the confusion is complete in a ballad of some twenty years later, where the coachman is unable to converse with his customers and can only babble forth in broken words, "Me no good Engalash." For this, and for the authorities from whom the above tale is narrated, see Appendix. For Bowman's in 1665, see next chapter ; also for John Painter, see Appendix. In "Anderson's Chronological Series," edition of 1784, we read : "1652, A coffee-house first opened in London." This is quite accurate. Anderson has also been quoted (though I have not found the reference) as stating that Pasqua took refuge in Holland.

coachman enjoyed the confidence of his customers to such a degree that they united in paying six-pence a-piece (to the number, it is said, of nearly a thousand), and in this manner he was enabled to convert his tent or booth into a house and to keep an apprentice at the trade. It will not be to our purpose at present to follow this particular business of Bowman's, which he left in a fair condition to his widow, who, it should be mentioned for the sake of completion, had formerly been Alderman Hodges' cook-maid.

At the second London coffee-house we meet with an old acquaintance who had long returned from his travels in the East, but had not forgotten the Turkish drink, "in taste a little bitterish ;" for "when coffee first came in," Sir Henry Blunt "was a great upholder of it, and hath ever since been a constant frequenter of coffee-houses, especially Mr. . . . Farre at the Rainbowe by Inner Temple gate."

Fleet Street has never been wanting in wonders, and here, at a later time, De Hightrehight "ate burning coals, swallowed flaming brimstone, and sucked a red-hot poker five times a day !"; yet the famous fire-eater did not perhaps excite any more wonder than our worthy knight with his

drink " of a soote colour, dryed in a Furnace, and
that they drinke as hote as can be endured." But
the neighbours of James Farr (who, by the way,
had formerly been a barber) did something more
than wonder at his new kind of enterprise, for in
the year 1657—probably his second year of business—he was by them presented (i.e. prosecuted)
" for makinge and selling of a drink called coffee,
whereby in makeing the same, he annoyeth his
neighbrs. by evil smells, and for keeping of
ffier for the most part night and day, whereby his
chimney and chambr. hath been sett on ffire, to
the great danger and affrightment of his neighbrs."
Three of the witnesses and complainants were
booksellers, and as one of these kept his shop in the
same building with Farr, we can well imagine his
fears lest the " drying-furnace" should lead to a
general conflagration. The prosecution comes
under the head of " Disorders and Annoys : " it is
not necessary to suppose that the tavern-keepers
were at the bottom of this opposition, or to exalt
the barber's character into that of a sufferer from
Puritan rigour; for, as Mr. Timbs observes, he
doubtless promised to mend the real nuisance of
his smoking chimney, and so was allowed to continue at the Rainbow, where we shall come across

him in later days after his success has produced many rivals.[1]

Sir Henry Blunt has some claims to be regarded as the father of English coffee-houses, for his strong individuality seems to have stamped itself upon the system. His favourite motto, " Loquendum est cum vulgo, sentiendum cum sapientibus," expresses well their colloquial purpose, and was natural enough on the lips of one whose experience had been world-wide. Though educated at Trinity College, Oxford, and at one time a collector of books, he was never a great reader, and much preferred club life to seclusion.

Aubrey, who praises his friend's clear judgment and "great foresight into government," narrates an incident which testifies no less to his personal courage than to his worldly wisdom. After his voyaging Sir Henry had returned to England and was a gentleman-pensioner in the service of Charles I. In this capacity he was present with the king at Edgehill fight, and afterwards at Oxford. Returning to London, he walked boldly into Westminster Hall with his sword by his side,

[1] See Appendix for further particulars respecting the booksellers at the Rainbow, and Aubrey's account of Sir Henry ; also for another version of the St. Alban's hoax.

to the great astonishment of the Parliamentarians. When called before the House of Commons to answer for his absence, his reply was that he had merely performed the duties of his office in attending upon his Majesty's person. Upon this strange plea of consistency Blunt was acquitted. The battle of Edgehill had not proved so decisive as to induce mere waverers to desert from the Royal Standard, yet we need not suppose that the knight was ever called upon to wait in his turn at court again. His opinions smacked somewhat strongly of Puritanism, for he was severe against titles, and wished to have every minister paid equally at the rate of one hundred pounds a year. He was not without serious faults in his private character, but, having been long an abstainer from intoxicating liquors, had acquired a habit of inveighing against the evils of drunkenness.

One trait in his character indicated a departure from the strictness of Puritan manners, viz. an inordinate love of joking; for the worthy knight "was heretofore a great *shammer*." The later "cock-and-bull" stories that found credit at coffee-houses were perhaps not more wonderful than a tale related with the utmost gravity by Sir Henry to the company assembled in the Rainbow. At a certain inn, said he, naming the sign, "the innkeeper had made a hogs'-trough of a free-stone coffin, but the pigges after that grew leane, dancing and skipping, and would run on the topps of the houses like goates." It is fair to add that this was a return shot for certain "stories that were very seldom true:" accordingly when the two young auditors (who are represented as being Jesuits in another version of the tale) came to the Rainbow next night, having just ridden back from St. Albans, where they had found the inn, but no trace of the pigs in question, Sir Henry Blunt was unabashed. They indeed looked leeringly upon him, and desired to know why he was not ashamed to tell such stories. He on his part asked whether they had really been to make inquiries, and, receiving for answer a solemn and indignant "yea," replied, "Why truly, gentlemen, I heard you tell strange things that I knew to be false. I would not have gone over the threshold of the dore to have found you in a lye." Thereupon the company fell to laughing at the two young gentlemen.

"Coffee and Commonwealth," says a pamphleteer of 1665, "came in together for a Reformation to make's a free and sober nation." The same writer (see Appendix) argues that liberty of speech should be allowed, "where men of differing judgments crowd;" "and," he adds, "that's a coffee-house, for where should men discourse so free as there?" Now perhaps we do not always connect the ideas of sociableness and freedom of discussion with the days of Puritan rule; yet it must be admitted that something like geniality and openness characterized what Pepys calls the Coffee Club of the Rota. This "free and open Society of ingenious gentlemen" was founded in the year 1659 by certain numbers of the Republican party, whose peculiar opinions had been timidly expressed and not very cordially tolerated under the Great Oliver. By the weak Government that followed these views were regarded with extreme dislike and, as we shall presently see, with some amount of terror.

They met, says Aubrey, who was himself of their number, at the Turk's Head in New Palace Yard, Westminster, "where they take water, the next house to the staires, at one Miles's, where was made purposely a large ovall table, with a passage in the middle for Miles to deliver his coffee." This curious refreshment-bar, and the interest with which the beverage itself was regarded, were quite secondary to the excitement caused by another novelty. When, after heated disputation, a member desired to test the opinion of the meeting, any particular point might by agreement be put to the vote, and then everything depended upon "our wooden oracle," the first balloting-box ever seen in England. Formal methods of procedure, and the intensely practical nature of the subjects discussed, combined to give a real importance to this Amateur Parliament. Aubrey, who long remembered their "ingeniose and smart discourses," declares that the arguments in the House itself "were but flatt to it." A due respect for minorities, and the certainty of being able to record an opinion without incurring pains and penalties, made this a more impartial assembly than that other which sat in daily fear in Westminster Hall. Of the prominent political characters included amongst its members, Aubrey, Pepys, and also Wood give lists (see Appendix). Some, e.g. "ye Earl Tirconnel, Sir John Penruddock, etc., Mr. John [afterwards Sir John] Birkenhead, . . . Stafford, Esq.," came for the purpose of upholding the opposite side in debate. Dr. William Petty was likewise "a Rota man," whose sentiments occasionally differed from those of the majority at the club. The opposition was not always of an orderly kind.

Aubrey tells how it was a common custom for members to adjourn to the Rhenish wine-house ; but on one occasion Mr. Stafford inverted the arrangement by coming with his companions " drunk from the taverne, and affronted the Junto ; the soldiers," i.e. officers, who, says Wood, were commonly there as auditors and spectators, " offered to kick them downe stayres, but Mr. Harrington's moderation and persuasion hindered it.   Mr. Stafford tore their orders and minutes."

The Mr. Harrington whose presence of mind prevented a scene, was well known as author of " Oceana," a work of genius, full of veiled political allusions that stood in some need of interpretation. James Harrington and his friend Henry Nevill had, even before the Rota was started, been in the habit of attending coffee-houses, where their "smart discourses and inculcations made many proselytes." Though the chair at the Rota was taken from time to time by various members, the society's chief occupation was to discuss those peculiar views concerning the balance of property which the founders held to be essential to the well-being of a commonwealth.   In fact the club took its name from Harrington's favourite scheme.   This was a device for obtaining machinery of government which should be free from the corruption of rust. Its officials would hold office temporarily. However, the Parliament need be never wholly new, though its members were constantly changing: "the third part of the house was to rote out by ballot every yeare." Henry Nevill was spokesman for the club in Parliament, and boldly predicted the ruin of that assembly unless his plans were adopted. The famous " Rump " clung tenaciously to their fragment of power, and we are not surprised to find that "the greatest part of the Parliament-men perfectly hated this designe of Rotation."

To further the cause Harrington published a long list of those whom he would have chosen as a Committee for the Reform of Parliament; amongst the names [1] occur his friend Henry Nevill, Major Wildman, Maximilian Petty, William Harrington, Praisegod Barebones, and our acquaintance of the Rainbow, Sir Henry Blunt. In order to ridicule this ambitious attempt, an unfriendly mimic put forth what he called the

---

[1] They were chosen with impartiality, and include " Mr. [Matt.] Wren " together with " Mr. Prynne," who published a reply to the proposal of "his Utopian excellency" and laughed at the " Puppet Play of a New Commonwealth."

"Decrees and Orders of the Committee of Safety of the Commonwealth of Oceana." Yet with the outside public the idea may have been momentarily popular. It seemed the only chance of abasing the "pride of senators for life," and of delivering the country from their insufferable tyranny. It anticipated General Monk's proposal for a Free Parliament, and that at a time when "to human foresight there was no possibility of the king's return."

At the beginning of Feb. 1659-60, Harrington penned a little tract called "The Rota; or, A Model of a Free State, or Equal Commonwealth: once proposed and debated in brief, and to be again more at large proposed to, and debated by, a free and open Society of ingenious Gentlemen." Pepys had been present at one of the preliminary debates, and his report shows that the excitement was like that of a sharply contested election.

"I went," he says, "on the 20th of January to the Coffee Club, and heard very good discourse; it was in answer to Mr. Harrington's answer, who said that the state of the Roman Government was not a settled Government, and so it was no wonder that the balance of propriety [i.e. property] was in one hand, and the command in another, it being therefore always in a posture of war; but it was carried by ballot that it was a steady Government, though it is true by the voices it had been carried before that it was an unsteady Government ; so to-morrow it is to be proved by the opponents that the balance lay in one hand, and the Government in another."

This bustling coffee club was probably never honoured by the august presence of Milton. Yet his interest was shown by the fact that " Mr. Cyriack Skinner, an ingeniose young gent. scholar to Jo Milton, was [sometimes] Chaire-man." About the time that Harrington's last-named booklet was produced, Milton wrote one with somewhat similar intent. The following is the humorous title of a pamphlet which was intended for the double purpose of casting a stone at Milton's politics and ridiculing those who were imagined to be his friendly critics :—

" The Censure of the Rota upon Mr. Miltons Book, entituled, The Ready and Easie way to Establish A Free Commonwealth.

" Die Lunae 26 Martii, 1660.

" Ordered by the Rota that M. Harrington be desired to draw up a Narrative of this dayes proceeding upon Mr. Milton's book . . . and to cause the same to be forthwith printed and pub shed, and a copy thereof to be sent to Mr. Milton.

" Trundle Wheeler, Clerk
to the Rota.

" Lon. Printed by Paul Giddy, Printer to the Rota, at the sign of the Windmill in Turne-againe Lane. 1660."

Though his initials are placed at the close, it is

hardly necessary to remark that this is no genuine production from the pen of James Harrington. A single quotation will suffice to show that whilst the writer is familiar with the more flighty style of speeches at the Rota, he is neither the author of " Oceana " nor one of his friends. A member of the club is made to say—

"That a Commonwealth is like a great Top, that must be kept up by being whipt round, and held in perpetuall circulation, for if you discontinue the Rotation, and suffer the Senate to settle, and stand still, down it falls immediately."

The club ceased to exist before the date mentioned in these its supposed minutes, and the shadow of coming events had cast a gloom over the society's latest proceedings. On the 20th of February, Pepys wrote :—

" After a small debate upon the question whether learned or unlearned subjects are best, the club broke up very poorly, and I do not think they will meet any more."

As we have seen, Harrington was to the last undismayed and even confident for the future. He uttered here his famous prophecy which, according to Hallam's definition of the phrase Common-wealthe's men (as including all those who opposed the King's Government), came so marvellously true :—

"He several times (at the breaking up) sayd, 'Well, the King will come in. Let him come in, and call a Parliament of ye greatest Cavaliers in England, so they be men of estates, and let them sett but 7 yeares, and they will all turn Common-wealthe's men."

Aubrey, who seems to have been present at the final gathering, says : —

"Well; this meeting continued Novemb. Dec. Jan. till Feb. 20 or 21, and then upon the unexpected turne upon Generall Monkes comeing in, all these airie modells vanished. Then 'twas not fitt, nay treason to have done such."

Long after its dissolution the club was remembered alike by friend and foe. It supplied Butler with the following illustration for his " Hudibras :"—

> "But Sidrophel as full of tricks
> As Rota men of Politicks."

Another " Censure of the Rota," in the year 1673, has been already noticed. The original club, or its Oxford imitation, was famed for literary strictures, as appears from a phrase in a pamphlet of the same year : to " damn beyond the fury of the Rota."

Of more significance than the mere survival of a name is the fact that Puritanism continued to modify the tone of coffee-house morals. In the following chapters we shall see the effects of this on manners and politics.

CHAPTER VI.

THE COFFEE-HOUSE AS A SOCIAL AND TEMPERANCE FACTOR.

" A Coffee House, the learned hold,
  It is a place where Coffee's sold ;
  This derivation cannot fail us,
  For where Ale's vended that's an Ale-house."—1665.

THE close connection between the social status of coffee-houses and their influence as a temperance institution, makes it desirable to devote a chapter to this twofold aspect. In discussing the question of the exclusion or admission of intoxicating liquors into these places, we shall cover the whole period from the year 1660 to the end of the seventeenth century. On the other hand, the story of the social development of coffee-houses falls naturally into two divisions, of which only the first, viz. the twenty-five years immediately following the Restoration, concerns us at present.

As regards the method adopted, I shall continue to make the reader free of the institution by means

of personal introductions to some of the chief
characters who were to be found there, whether
as guests or as hosts. This manner of tracing the
growth of the London coffee-house implies a
reference to the early broadsides and minute contemporary criticisms which hailed its introduction.
Nor are such antiquarian details unnecessary, or
intended merely to serve as an effective background to the picture. Of eight tracts upon the
subject (written between the Restoration and the
year 1675), no less than four have the words
"Character of a Coffee-house" as part of their
title. These were no mere fancy descriptions, for
their authors seemed really anxious to impart a
knowledge of the town's latest novelty, which
many readers had not as yet seen for themselves.
This kind of first-hand evidence is limited in
quantity; there presently came a time when fresh
information was no longer needed, the average
Londoner had only to step to the end of his
particular street in order to find a specimen, and
judge by his own experience of its merits or
demerits.

One of these early pamphlets professes to give
the dialogue between "a learned Knight and a
pitifull Pedagogue," and contains an amusing

account of a house where the Puritan element
is still in the ascendant. A numerous company
is present, and each little group being occupied
with its own subject, the general effect is that of a
mere Babel. Whilst one is engaged in quoting
the classics, another confides to his neighbours
how much he admires Euclid:—

> " A third's for a Lecture, a fourth a Conjecture,
>   A fifth for a penny in the pound."

Even Theology is introduced: Masques, Balls,
and Plays are condemned. Others again discuss
the news, and are deep in the "store of Mercuries
here to be found:" one cries up Philosophy,
and—

> " Whether Harrington's Rota or Boyl's Virtuosa
>   Be the nobler design they determine."

Pedantry is rife, and for the most part unchecked,
when each 'Prentice-boy " doth call for his coffee
in Latin," and all are so prompt with their learned
quotations that " 't'would make a poor Vicar to
tremble."

The stranger having once accustomed himself
to the din and multitude of subjects, would next
be surprised at the strange variety of social com-
binations which the coffee-house presented. Accordingly a rhymster of 1665, in depicting the

humours of the place, has amongst his characters
a griping usurer, a player full fine, an ill-tempered
Puritan, a Virtuoso, and a Country Bumpkin.
For purposes of observation it is likened to the
"top of Paul's High Steeple:" from that post of
vantage the whole city was to be viewed, and
"even so all people may here be seen." Another
writer makes use of a still bolder metaphor in
describing the universal resort: it is a rota-room,
and, like Noah's ark, receives every kind of creature, "from the precise diminutive band to the
hectory cravat and cuffs in folio."

In this last "Character of a Coffee-house" we
have representatives of very different classes in
society. The town wit now appears upon the
scene; likewise there are present a grave citizen,
worthy lawyer, worshipful justice, reverend non-
conformist, and voluble sailor, whose name, "Captain All-man-sir," reminds us of Bunyan's pilgrims.
In the critic's imagination the coffee-house is a
lay conventicle, its cheer is "good fellowship
turned puritan;" all who resort thither are "Le-
vellers;" and to complete the motley group we
have "an errant thief" and the "bully rook,"
whose sole object is to entice his hapless victim
into a neighbouring tavern.

However, the writer depicts a lively scene that sometimes occurs in the coffee-house. If any enthusiast raises his voice and shows signs of unusual wit or eloquence, he presently becomes the centre of an admiring group, with the result that " the further tables are abandoned ; and all the rest flock round." On such occasions the impassioned talker will hold his audience spellbound, until the very existence of their pipes is forgotten, and the coffee itself is suffered to grow cold !

In " Coffee-houses Vindicated " we find not so much an answer as a panegyric, and " spight of the idle sarcasms " the system is shown to have many advantages. It is the sanctuary of health, the delight of frugality, an academy of civility, a sort of finishing school which will put an excellent polish upon the manners, as it is able to cure the *pudor subrusticus*, i.e. " clownish kind of modesty frequently incident to the best natures." Against the aspersion that these places were gossip-mongers' halls, the writer sets up a curious defence, and one that may perhaps be presented as a specimen of coffee-house argument. He quotes the proverb concerning prating by way of excuse, as if in consideration of the superior wisdom of such places Solomon himself were making an allowance for occasional reaction : no one can be at all times wise, therefore "*in multiloquio non deest vanitas.*"

Close intercourse between the various *habitués* of a coffee-house was to lead to something better than what it appeared at first, a mere jumbling or huddling together of opposites. We shall presently see how diverse elements gradually united in the bonds of common sympathy, or were forcibly combined by persecution from without, until there resulted a social, political, and moral force of almost irresistible strength.

Meanwhile the Puritan began by scorning " all complements and gentile breeding," and rejoiced to meet where none to other need give place. The simplicity of the primitive institution is well illustrated by the following " Rules and Orders of the Coffee-house" appended to the " Brief Description of . . . that sober and wholesome drink," bearing date 1674 (see Ch. IV. p. 57, and Bibliography). Similar regulations may have been hung up in Puritan houses before that year ; it would, however, be difficult to fix upon a time when politics were really regarded with such decent respect, to say nothing of wagers limited to five shillings, and healths which might not be drunk with impunity even in coffee.[1]

"THE RULES AND ORDERS OF THE COFFEE HOUSE.

"Enter sirs freely, But first if you please,
Peruse our Civil-Orders, which are these.
First, Gentry, Tradesmen, all are welcome hither,
And may without affront sit down together:
Pre-eminence of place, none here should mind,
But take the next fit seat that he can find:
Nor need any, if Finer Persons come,
Rise up to assigne to them his room;
To limit men's Expence, we think not fair,
But let him forfeit Twelve-pence that shall swear:
He that shall any Quarrel here begin,
Shall give each man a Dish t' atone the sin;
And so shall he, whose Complements extend
So far to drink in COFFEE to his Friend;
Let Noise of loud disputes be quite forborn,
No Maudlin Lovers here in corners mourn,
But all be brisk, and talk, but not too much.
On Sacred Things, let none presume to touch,
Nor profane Scripture, nor saucily wrong
Affairs of State with an irreverent tongue:
Let mirth be innocent, and each man see
That all his jests without reflection be;
To keep the House more quiet and from blame,
We banish hence Cards, Dice and every Game:
Nor can allow of Wages that exceed
Five shillings, which oft-times much trouble breed,
Let all that's lost, or forfeited, be spent
In such Good Liquor as the House doth vent,

---

[1] Cf. their custom of drinking healths by stratagem: "Do thou take another cup, and I will do likewise, and let us wish each other well" (*Tait's Magazine*, n.s. 22: 104).

> And Customers endeavour to their powers,
> For to observe still seasonable hours.
> Lastly, let each man what he calls for Pay,
> And so you're welcome to come every day."

This patronage by the Puritan, whose party badges were no longer in favour, though it exercised an important influence upon the after history of coffee-houses, was rather insinuated as an objection than acknowledged. Nor could such a despised connection in any way help to make the institution generally acceptable. In order to explain what was both a sudden and unexpected increase of popular favour, it is well to remember that the love of change introduced at the Restoration was by no means confined to a question of politics. Everything old-fashioned seems to have been at a discount, whilst to appear new-fangled or foreign meant instant popularity. The upheaval of opinion showed itself by a common desire for change in such matters as food and dress. With this humour the advocates of coffee-houses hastened to comply; one writer issues free invitations as to a place where folk may learn the latest fashions :—

> " How perrewigs are curl'd ;
> And for a penny you shall heare,
> All novells in the world."

Another, writing in no friendly spirit, is compelled to admit that the " Knack begins to mode,
and it sells quick as the new perukes nowadays ;"
for like " the fashion of your cloathes, you change
. . . your drink as often to as new and strange."
The same writer attempts to stem the tide of
novelty, and cries shame on the notion that Englishmen should imitate the Turk :—

> " For men and 'Xtians to turn Turks, and think
> T' excuse the crime because 'tis in their drink,
> Is more than Magick. . . .
> Pure English Apes ! ye may, for ought I know,
> Would it but mode, learn to eat spiders too." [1]

---

[1] We have never imported the Chinese edible spider ;
yet, as Isaac D'Israeli says, this witty poet was not without
a degree of prescience in speaking of the luxury, for
Monsieur Lalande, the French astronomer, with one or
two humble imitators have triumphed over prejudice and
were epicures of this stamp. The above broadside, " A
Cup of Coffee, or Coffee in its Colours," was published in
1663.

This rage for foreign productions did not grow less
towards the end of Charles's reign. At that time a grumbler
finds fault with " little Sparks who scorn to eat, drink, or
wear anything that comes not from France or the Indies,"
and he would have his eager countrymen profit by the
example of " the most Acute and Ingenious Ambassador
from the Emperor of Fez and Morocco (who now resides
amongst us)," for his attendants were " to see everything
but admire nothing," less they should appear to disparage
their own country and show themselves ignorant of the

When inclined to be critical our author does not shrink from using epithets; he first confesses ignorance of this "loathsome potion not yet understood," and then corrects himself by the following analysis :—

> "Syrop of soot and Essence of old shoes
> Dasht with Diurnals and the Books of News."

But the most absurd part of this diatribe is that in which the ghosts of Ben Jonson and his comrades are supposed upon the scene : these worthies at the sight of coffee, "fleeing, cry out, Sulphur, Liquid Fire," and are terribly shocked at the sad falling off which the Stuart customs show from the good old days when they drank "pure nectar sublimed with rich canary in their clubs :"—

> "Should any of your grandsires ghosts appear
> In your wax-candle circles and but hear
> The name of coffee so much called upon
>
> .   .   .   .   .
>
> Would they not startle think ye."

Curiously enough the very Orders of a coffee-house which we have lately been quoting are to some extent a reproduction of the actual words of "Ben Johnsons sociable rules for the Apollo," as

wonders of Barbary. "The Natural History of Coffee . . . with a Tract of Elder and Juniper-Berries, shewing how useful they may be in our Coffee-Houses," 1682.

given in the English translation by Alexander Brome (2nd edition of his " Songs and Poems "). There the company are told to have a care " that all our jests without reflection be:" they are warned that after a full repast " on serious things, or sacred," none should touch : and in the same spirit of fraternity counsel is given that " none contend who shall sit high or low." This idea of imitating the Elizabethan heroes was not merely accidental. In "the Oxford Coffee-Academy instituted by Apollo," to which reference has been made in the last chapter, one of the characters was " a grave gentleman that us'd to sup in Apollo and could tell many storys of Ben Johnson." The protest of that worthy, had he been able to revisit his former haunts, would doubtless have been against the heavy drinking and unbounded licence which excluded sense from the company, and rendered the old wit-combats no longer possible.

Nor can we suppose a great need of instruction in this art of hard drinking at a time when " the merry monarch " was himself issuing proclamations against bibulous followers who persisted in " giving no other evidence of their affection towards us but in drinking our health."

Whilst the new invention retained so much of the former social traditions as to move to envy the mind of our pamphleteer, the truth is that, unlike the first establishments of similar name in France, these earliest London coffee houses were distinct from, and in the main opposed to, the tavern and the ale-house.[1]

It is, moreover, desirable to mark very clearly the distinction between seventeenth century coffee houses, with which alone this book is concerned, and those of later date. Having the more illustrious name—frequented as they were by the brightest literary " stars " of each successive reign —the coffee houses that come after the Revolution would require a bookshelf to themselves, or rather, they do already occupy an important place in every great library. Yet with all their brilliance they have not so much connected interest, are not so important as an institution, and never enjoyed the

[1] Since writing the above I have had the pleasure of seeing Mr. W. C. Sydney's " Social Life in England, 1660–1690." On page 424 Mr. Sydney says, " The taverns of London in the second half of the seventeenth century were in marked contrast to the coffee houses. Within the walls of the latter there was always much noise, much clatter, much bustle, but decency was never outraged." The reader will do well to consult for himself the pages (409–423) of that interesting book which deal specially with our subject.

same kind of political and even national importance as their more humble and more genuine
predecessors.

It would be absurd to imagine that at any time
an ideal perfection was reached in all places where
they provided "a fashionable mess of Turkish
sobriety." Knowing full well how the flood of
rioting and intoxication carried almost everything
away, it must be admitted that at their best the
coffee houses were not an all-sufficient barrier;
that in some instances they readily opened their
doors to dissipation; and that at a later period,
when the evil had assumed a new form, they were
worse than undone, and continued only as a hollow
mockery of their former purpose.

Yet by confining our attention to the earlier
period we may see a ray of light in what is generally regarded as the dreariest passage in the
history of the morals of the English people.
Coffee houses had undoubtedly fallen upon evil
days, and incurred the hearty dislike of all those
who were impatient of restraint. But this ill-will
was itself an evidence that they were in their
sociable manner no small restraint upon the evil,
whilst indeed they eventually proved one of the
means by which the middle classes of society were

enabled to pass through that time of dissipation almost unharmed.

In order that a claim of this sort may be decided with fairness, it is necessary to enter into the somewhat conflicting details of contemporary evidence; and, witnesses being summoned from amongst foes as well as friends, the reader must please to consider himself as judge of the merits of the case.

Of James Howel's testimony there is no reason to be ashamed, for he takes evident delight in expressing his opinion of the twofold benefit conferred. After saying how " 'tis found already that this coffee drink hath caused a greater sobriety among the Nations," he adds an explanation of the wonder:—

" Whereas formerly Apprentices and clerks with others used to take their morning's draught in Ale, Beer, or Wine, which, by the dizziness they Cause in the Brain, made many unfit for business, they use now to play the Good-fellows in this wakeful and civil drink : Therefore that worthy gentleman, Mr. Muddiford, who introduced the practice hereof first to London, deserves much respect of the whole Nation." [1]

---

[1] Extract from letter published by Judge Rumsey in his " Organon ;" see edition of 1664. In the State Papers, Domestic Series, 1653, is a letter to the Ambassador at Constantinople, which thanks him for resisting " the Jew's

The mournful critic who was so taken aback at the notion of the club meeting elsewhere than at an ale-house, likewise regarded it as " the very head and front " of its offending, that the new fashion should venture "for the Vine's pure blood " to substitute a something " not yet understood." Yet another pamphleteer of the preceding year had said with enthusiasm of mine host :—

> " Good coffee he draws and shirbets because
>   They'r pleasant and sweet chockalet,"

adding with a note of triumph "no sack is here drunk." In similar doggerel we are told a few years later,—

> " The drinking here of Chocolate
>   Can make a fool a sophie ;"

and, as if to make the parallel complete, this same verse concludes with the invitation :—

pretence upon Mr. Modiford." Roger North tells how, whenever a fresh merchant came to this city, the first Jew that caught a word with him marked him for his own, and, sticking " like a burr," so contrived it that no business could be done without his services, which were those of a universal broker. It is likely that the victim, being loosed from his Jewish persecutor, returned to England, and became one of the earliest patrons of the coffee house. The spelling of this name varies. I have found also Murford, Mudford, Moundeford, and a Thomas Modyford was Prize Commissioner at the Barbadoes in 1655.

> " Then let us to the coffee house go,
>   'Tis cheaper far than wine."

Nothing, however, could be more to our purpose, or more pithily expressed, than the verdict of a writer of the year 1665, whose " Character of a Coffee house " we shall presently (in the *Appendix*, see also p. 106) quote more fully :—

> " A coffee house the learned hold,
>   It is a place where Coffee's sold;
>   This derivation cannot fail us,
>   For where Ale's vended, that's an Ale-house."

We next come to the testimony of a coffee-man named Elford, who has preserved to us one memorable scene from the days of his boyhood, whilst the story of his own life furnishes a clue to the somewhat puzzling statements that he makes about the kind of drink supplied in these places. Elford's father had won an early renown by inventing the white iron machine for roasting coffee, " since much used, and which is turn'd on a spit by a Jack." The son was himself in the business until some few years after the Revolution, and it was his belief that neither tea nor chocolate were sold in these places before that event, whilst at the time of his own retirement " Drams and Cordial Waters were to be had only at coffee houses newly set up, the old standers still refusing to admit them." It is easy to imagine that in some instances the new drink would not allow of a rival, and Dr. Douglas says that, at the price of a penny halfpenny per dish, so great was the demand that coffee-men were obliged to make it in pots of eight or ten gallons. He adds, probably upon Elford's authority, that it was a great while after the Fire of London before they thought of selling anything there except coffee and "a certain Composition call'd Aromatick, recommended by Physicians ; and a Liquor made with Betony, for the sake of such as could not accustom themselves to the bitter taste of coffee ; for few people then mix'd it with either sugar or milk." [1]

By means of contemporary advertisements we are able to test the accuracy of Elford's statement,

[1] See " Coffee Tree," part ii. p. 33. The drink was at one time mixed with sugar candy or even mustard. Another very early substitute, called Bocket by John Houghton, was a concoction of sassafras and sugar. This was revived in later times, and Lamb (Essay on " Chimney-Sweepers ") speaks of it under the name of Saloop, as wood boiled down to a kind of tea and tempered with an infusion of milk and sugar. He did not venture to dip his own " peculiar lip " in the mixture, yet had known palates " not uninstructed in dietetical elegancies sup it with avidity "—and it may well have been superior to the " something sweet and something hot," misnamed of coffee nowadays !

and obtain some curious references to the business
of a coffee-man as it was conducted before the
Great Fire. At that time, Constantine Jennings,
or George Constantine, as Dr. Douglas calls him,
of the " Grecian," not only advertised his chocolate,
sherbet, and tea, but was offering gratuitous instruction in the art of preparing these liquors.[1]
His coffee house was from very early days frequented by certain members of the Royal Society,
who seem to have met here as a committee, on their
return from Gresham College, and were called "the
Learned Club." Doubtless these worthies would
patronize each of the newly-imported drinks in
turn, by way of scientific experiment. We may
notice in passing that the host himself had begun
his life as a seafaring man, and originally set
up for English customers in Wapping, ultimately
moving to Devereux Court, where his name was
still to be seen on the sign of the Grecian in the

---

[1] The *Intelligencer*, January 23rd, 1664–5 : " One *Constantine* a *Grecian*, living in *Thredneedle-street*, over against *St.
Christophers Church, London,* being licensed to sell and
retail Coffee, Chocolate, Cherbert, and Tea, desires it to be
notified, that the right *Turky* Coffee Berry or Chocolate
may be had as cheap and as good of him the said *Constantine* at the place aforesaid, as is anywhere to be had for
mony : And that people may there be taught to prepare
the said Liquors gratis."

year 1727. In that year he was able to supplement Elford's testimony concerning the trade, and Dr. Douglas calls him "the oldest coffeeman now alive in London, and perhaps in Christendom." Even admitting that the account which describes him as the only man "who for fourteen years made coffee for the Great Bashaw" was a humorous exaggeration, yet he lived for more than sixty years after taking up his abode at the Grecian, and must, in his later days, have become a living witness to the fact that coffee and its kindred beverages in no way interfered with longevity. It is curious that in the very alley where Elford's father kept a coffee house an energetic neighbour was driving a brisk trade in chocolate, also "sherbets made in Turkie, of lemons, roses, and violets perfumed; and Tea or Chaa, according to its goodness." Another announcement of this same coffee house is to the effect that intending customers "are invited (the first day of the next new year) at the Signe of the Great Turk at the new Coffee house in Exchange Alley, where coffee will be on free cost, and so may be to the world's end."[1] This expectation of a long con-

Kingdom's *Intelligencer*, 1662. The former advertisement is here quoted from Timb's "Clubs," p. 347; it

tinuance was to be disappointed by the calamities which shortly befell the city.

Yet even the Plague itself could not entirely crush the social instincts of a Londoner, and Elford —who was at this time a schoolboy—tells us of a scene that often occurred in the coffee-room up the first flight of stairs at Bowman's. Some folk still ventured to seek out the old place of cheerful intercourse. No longer did any converse freely with strangers; and, having upon entrance "looked quite round the room," they would only join in company with acquaintances when an all-important question had been asked concerning the health of friends left at home. If all was well they sat down together, but in the case of the least uncertainty they would keep apart from one another, drinking in solitude, and, as it were, by stealth.[1]

This our last glimpse at social life in the "oulde coffee house formerly Bowman's," being a vivid scrap of recollection, may be contrasted with the riot and disorder of that Houndsditch tavern club

is also given in Burn's "Trade Tokens," p. 68. See Appendix and Illustration for "Tokens."

[1] "Coffee Tree," part ii. p. 30, In the "Orders conceived and published by the Lord Mayor at this time, it is commanded "that disorderly Tippling in Taverns, Alehouses, Coffee Houses and Cellars be severely looked into."

in which Defoe's genius has focused the despair
of those who abandoned hope at this terrible crisis·

The disaster of September, 1666, led to some
confusion in the crowded neighbourhood of the
Exchange, and when the ground came again to be
built upon, "Mr. Garraway, by some means or
other, got into the same place where Elford had
been, and there opened the first coffee house after
the Fire." The last-named was unable to regain
what had probably been only a single room up-
stairs. He presently reopened in George Yard,
leading into St. Michael's Alley, in which Pasqua
and Bowman had once set up their coffee tent and
shed, and this new establishment was called after
his own name.[1]

[1] It afterwards obtained the reputation of being the earliest
coffee house in London ; but the ground on which Bowman's
had stood was probably occupied by the " Virginia," and,later
on, by the " Jamaica." The map shows that this last was
damaged by the fire of 1748, which consumed the two rival establishments, viz., Elford's and Garraway's. Though its date
is quite outside our period, the map will also give an idea of
the many coffee houses that clustered round the Exchange,
and, in several instances, took their names from the various
" Walks " of the merchants. John's and Hain's were in
Birchin Lane ; Lloyd's was in Lombard Street, at the corner
of Abchurch Lane. 'Change Alley, says Burn, was but a
narrow passage, and in the disposition of the new sites had,
after the fire of 1666, still a confined space, till Alderman
Backwell's house in Lombard Street was demolished.

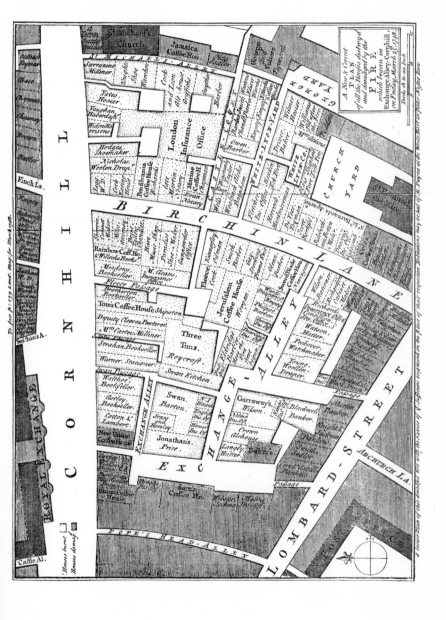

Elford's successor put forth a shop bill, describing himself as " Tobacconist and Retailer of Tea and Coffee," and in this he claims to have sold tea at a very early date. It runs thus :—

" Tea in England hath been sold in the leaf for 6 pounds and sometimes for 10 pounds the lb. weight, and in respect of its former scarceness and dearness, it hath been only used as a regalia in high treatments and entertainments, and presents made thereof to princes and grandees till the year 1657. The said Thomas Garway did purchase a quantity thereof, and first publicly sold the said tea in leaf and drink, &c."

The bill is without date of publication, and, though it was issued from some place in Exchange Alley, we cannot tell whether its issuer had as yet succeeded Elford. It affords no certain proof that Garraway was in the coffee trade before the Great Fire ; and even if he really introduced the Chinese drink as early as 1657, we cannot accept the common statement that "tea was first sold in England here," i.e. in the house which he is only known to have entered some ten years afterwards. A bitter feeling, caused by the after-success of his rival, shows itself in Elford's narrative, and perhaps explains his attempt to define a coffee-man as one who refused to sell anything else but coffee.[1]

[1] There is abundant proof that Elford is incorrect in his statement regarding the sale of tea and chocolate in these

So far was the average coffee-man from confining himself to one or two particular drinks, that the beverages were often miscellaneous as the company. The author of "Hudibras" has described him as keeping—

"A coffee market, where people of all qualities and conditions meet to trade in foreign drinks and newes, ale, smoak, and controversy. He admits of no distinction of persons, but gentleman, mechanic, lord, and scoundrel mix, and are all of a piece, as if they were resolved into their first principles."

The same point is made clear by the evidence of a foreigner who seems to have been at remarkable

places. In this respect the London houses resembled the earliest started at Oxford (see Chap. V. p. 73). An advertisement in the *Mercurius Politicus* (September 23rd to September 30th, 1658) runs thus :—"That Excellent and by all Physitians approved, *China* Drink, called by the *Chineans*, *Teha*, by other nations *Tay alias Tee*, is sold at the Sultaness-head, *a Cophee-house* in *Sweetings* Rents by the Royal Exchange, *London*." Likewise in *Rugge's Mercurius Politicus Redivivus* for November, 1659, we are told "there was also at this time a Turkish drink to be sould, almost in every street, called Coffee, and another kind of drink called Tee, and a drink called charcolate, which was a very harty drink." [For Token of the Sultaness Coffee House, see Illustration and Appendix. The latter quotation is from the MS. in the British Museum. Garway's bill and other curious documents relating to our subject are most readily to be found there by referring to the "Old General Catalogue."]

pains to pry into remote corners of London. Some
thirty different kinds of drink were sold in the
ale-houses and taverns, says our informant, who is
supposed to have been the Florentine Ambassador.
In coffee-houses were to be found—

> " Other beverages such as chocolate, sherbet, tea, ale,
> cock-ale, beer, &c., according to the season. In these there
> are diverse rooms, or meeting places of newsmongers, where
> one hears all that is, or is thought to be, news, true or false.
> In winter to sit round a large fire and smoke for two hours
> costs but 2 soldi (= 2*d.*) ; if you drink you pay besides for
> all that you consume."

Perhaps the pipes and tobacco were not included
in this modest account of an Ambassador's ex-
penses ! [1]

Whilst, however, intoxicating liquors are not
entirely excluded from either of the above lists
they do not seem to have become an item of importance for many years, and we have direct

---

[1] "Antiquary," vol. ii. p. 9. Mr. J. Theodore Bent thinks
it probable that this account was written in 1669. For the
extract from Butler's " unpublished remains " see " Antiquary," vol. iv. p. 140 ; Butler died in the year 1680.
Misson in 1698 says likewise of these places :—" On y boit
une tasse de caffé ou de quelque autre chose." This last re-
calls the delightful addition to Sir Walter Raleigh's exploits
in " Comic Sketches from English History : "—

> " One morning he sat in his study at ease
> Enjoying his coffee, *or what you may please.*"

evidence that wine and spirits were not freely
admitted at two of the most prominent places.
We shall have occasion to add something concerning the fashionable repute of Man's, and the
literary distinctions of Will's famed establishment,
but for the present it need only be observed that
they were much-frequented houses of entertainment.

From "An Exact and True Narrative of the
Popish Intrigue" we learn, upon the information of
a foreigner, given in court, that in the year 1679—

"A gentleman, who called himself Mr. Wyard, came to
this Informant at Will's Coffee-House and spake very kindly
to this Informant, and desired this Informant to go to the
tavern and drink a glass of wine with him; which this
Informant consented unto, and went out of the Coffee House
with him, and desired him to go to the Rose Tavern "—in
the same street.

A similar incident is related, at a still later time, as
taking place in Man's Coffee House, and one might
fancy that "the London Spy" had himself been
present during the trial. The Flatterer employs a
like device : praising his victim's shallow sense,
whilst, in return, "the idiot admires his fawning
eloquence." They are also obliged to leave the
coffee house in order to satisfy their desires in the
matter of strong drink :—

> " And that he further may enjoy
> A man of such Desert,
> He steps to Locket's 'cross the way,
> And Treats him with a Quart."

Instead of needlessly multiplying quotations, we may content ourselves with glancing at what the rival pamphlets of 1673 and 1675 have to say upon this subject. The former shows that to fully relish the peculiar flavour of the coffee drink, to forget its dark and murky colour, and to grow accustomed to its "scalding" properties, has required an education of the taste. The country bumpkin could not, upon first coming up to town, take kindly to "Pluto's diet drink," now offered him in the place of his beloved ale and cider.

As regards those who came regularly from the tavern to the coffee house, the writer seems to think that the object was not to prevent possible harm to their constitutions, but to repair their reputations by purchasing, "at the expense of their last penny, the repute of sober companions." To please all palates was the coffee-man's endeavour; accordingly he provided—

" Tea and aromatick for the sweet-toothed gentleman, betony and rosade . . . chocolate for the consumptive gallant,[1] Herefordshire readstreak made of rotten apples at

---

[1] In Brown's " Amusements " (published in 1700) there is

the Three Cranes, true Brunswick mum brewed at St. Catharine's, and ale in penny mugs, not so big as a taylor's thimble."

In reply, it is suggested that this abusive pamphleteer was "more conversant somewhere else than in coffee houses." These last are called "a sanctuary of health and nursery of temperance." It is argued that commercial matters cannot be properly conducted in an ale-house, where the continued sipping, "though never so warily," flies at last to the head. The use of the new institution as an appointment-room for men of business should prevent this constant muddling of the brain :—

"If people would be persuaded to play the good fellows in this wholesome, wakeful, innocent drink, they would find it do no less good to their bodies, and much more promote and advance their business and employments."

The true interest of this latter pamphlet certainly consists in its careful recognition of the part which

a mention of "a Beau that has play'd away his Estate at a Chocolate House," and a reference to "a Chocolate House in Covent Garden" where gaming was practised. However, at that date (according to the same critic), "To the Charms of Coffee, the wiser sort joyn'd Spirit of Clary, Usquebaugh, and Brandy," in the coffee house. North's "Examen" likewise speaks of the ill-use of coffee houses being "much improved by a new Invention called Chocolate Houses . . . where Gaming is added . . . as if the Devil had erected a new University."

the coffee house is to play in the struggle between Intemperance and Sobriety. When it speaks of "the ill habit of extraordinary drinking grown too epidemical amongst us," we may take the phrase in its literal sense, for the fashionable excess introduced at the Restoration had spread amongst the people like a plague.

We may conclude our twofold argument by noticing what Pepys has to say upon this subject, the very presence of the diarist being enough to show that, from a social point of view, the coffee house was not to be despised.

It is quite needless to do more than call attention to the contradictory elements in the character of Pepys. He was regarded by his contemporaries as an eminently practical man of business, proving a trustworthy and useful public servant, and receiving not unmerited favour from the king and Duke of York. He also became a member of Parliament, and at a still later time was held in such esteem as to be made President of the Royal Society. Yet the publication of his minute and copious diary has placed us behind the scenes, and presents him in a very different and often unfavourable light. Boswell's portraiture of his own failings is quite self-laudatory and dignified when compared with Pepys' confessions of inner littleness.[1] To take but a single example—and one which reminds us that his post was never deserted during this or the coming disaster—in the midst of the year of horror we find him idly wondering what would be the new fashion in head-dress, to take the place of periwigs, as soon as the plague should have abated. We may perceive him likewise trifling in the presence of a different kind of danger, and only half-conscious of the 'wickedness in high places,' which yet he minutely records. Upon glancing over the voluminous sheets of the diary, it seems strange that such an one as by his own confession he was, should have ever held up his head in that whirlpool of dissipation. At times, indeed, he began to share in the more dangerous kind of pleasures. On a certain occasion he is unable to occupy his place at the head of his household lest it should be perceived that the master had been over-indulging in strong drink. Evenings spent

[1] See a lively description of " Pepys and the World he lived in," by Henry B. Wheatley, F.S.A. It is suggested by Sir W. Scott, in his comments on Lord Braybrooke's edition (from which, for the most part, I have quoted), that Pepys' character was considerably modified in later years. He was only thirty-seven years old when, through failing eyesight, he had to close his diary, which was written in cipher.

in such excess are followed by nights of dis-
comfort, and on the morrow he is unable to do
aught but fiddle, to the sad neglect of more
prosaic duties. Or again, his friends assure him
that the best cure for headache is by a return to
the liquor that wrought the harm. But though
the secret of the change must to some extent
remain a secret, it is clear that he was advised, on
account of his rapidly-failing health, "to avoid
drinking often," and in the diary we are allowed
to see something of the manner of reformation. Walking up and down in Temple Gardens
on a "Lord's Day," we find him, book in hand,
engaged in reading the oaths which he had taken
against "drinking of wine and going to plays."
Even Pepys could be serious for an hour! He had
commenced in a practical way by resolving to
drink no wine for a week, "finding it unfit me to
look after business." This attempt at self-control
was partially successful; and later on he again
records how the resolution "keeps me most happily
and contentedly to my business." Pepys had no
distaste for theatres, and his partial abstention was
chiefly due to economical fears; witness the following entry for November 13, 1667 :—

"To my chamber, and do begin anew to bind myself to

keep my old vows, and among the rest not to see a play till Christmas but once in every other week, and have laid aside 10*l.* which is to be lost to the poor if I do."

Surely the needy were not uncared for that winter!

It is also true that a somewhat elastic conscience made use of many a trifling excuse. Whereas he is at one time glad of money instead of wine, and sells off his hogsheads of sherry, at another he is boasting that his cellar contains more canary and sack than that of any who had borne the family name before him. When the oaths are out he keeps neither from wine nor playhouse, though, of course, he is only "taking a liberty to-day" with intent "to fall to them again!" At a city feast in the Guildhall his vow was something worse than broken, if, at least, we are to reject Pepys' plea of ignorance concerning the ingredients of the "medicated wine" of Hippocrates: "Wine was offered," says the diarist on the 29th of October, 1663, "and they drunk, I only drinking some hippocras, which do not break my vowe, it being only a mixed compound drink, and not any wine."

Sir Walter Scott matches what he calls this piece of bacchanalian casuistry with "Fielding's Chaplain of Newgate, who preferred punch to wine, because the former was a liquor nowhere spoken against in Scripture."

When he came to be less frequent at the tavern and the wine-drinking, Pepys made some really honest attempts to find a substitute. Sir William Batten, his friend and adviser, who, however, is not always respectfully mentioned in the diary, presents him with three bottles of his essence water. Pepys now notices for the first time "the juice of oranges with sugar, drunk as wine:" he sends (on September 25th, 1660), for "a cup of tee (a China drink), of which I never had drank before." Chocolate is also tried, and at the New Exchange he drinks whey, "with much entreaty getting it for our money, and they would not be entreated to let us have one glasse more."

It was just at this critical time that Pepys was wont to resort most often to the coffee houses, and we may there, by means of his own descriptions, picture him after he had adopted the cavalier fashions, having on his silken coat of the golden buttons, or perhaps with belt and silver-hilted sword, or, again, as he appeared one morning at the end of November, arrayed in the "best black cloth suit, trimmed with scarlet ribbon, very neat, with my cloak lined with velvett, and a new beaver,

which altogether is very noble." [1] When invited
out to dine, and at a loss for a more pleasant way
of whiling away the time until noon, he takes a
coach, and, in company with Sir W. Batten, drives
in state to the coffee house in Cornhill, which he
finds, as usual, full of company and much talk.
At the Globe, in Fleet Street, he listens with
delight to a young fellow, "a pretty man and a
Parliament man," who is doubtless practising eloquence and getting up his reputation for smart
repartee. On another occasion he is diverted by
the simple discourse concerning Quakers, said to be
charmed with strings about their wrists. Again,
it amuses him to hear how lightly the Presbyterians
can talk in the cheerful atmosphere of the coffee
house, though their cause is well-nigh desperate
out of doors. After paying a shilling to stand on
the wheel of a cart at a crowded execution, he
retires to a coffee house, where the style and subject
of discourse can easily be imagined. He is entertained at one of these "schools for scandal" by the
account of a rich young widow, said to be worth

[1] To this description Pepys adds:—"With my black silk
knit canons [knee ornaments] which I bought a month ago."
On the next day (December 1st) he went to Whitehall pre-
sumably in this gorgeous attire, and thence at noon to the
coffee house.

about 80,000*l.*, and for whom the courtiers are
making somewhat interested inquiries. Yet graver
topics were by no means excluded. Besides telling
of several first-rate and scientific talkers who frequented these informal assemblies, Pepys gives an
enthusiastic account of one of the discussions in
which he himself took part. The subject was that
much-canvassed question of our own days as to
which are the very best books. Three had then
the well-nigh universal suffrage, being "most generally esteemed and cried up for wit," viz. Sir
Thomas Browne's "Religio Medici," Osborne's
"Advice to a Son," and the recently-published
"Hudibras." Whilst Pepys himself tells us concerning this last, "It hath not a good liking in me,"
the chief disputant of the coffee house, who was
William Petty, of Rota fame,[1] vehemently denounced

---

[1] See Chapter V. (p. 97). Dr. Petty, afterwards Sir William,
was amongst the Oxonians who formed the nucleus of the
Royal Society. Pepys here calls his friend "one of the
most rational men that ever I heard speak with tongue."
Sir G. Ascue was also present at this discussion (January
27th, 1663-4). Petty once told Evelyn that when in " a great
streight for money" at Paris, he had lived for " a week on
two penniworth (or three, I have forgott which, but I should
thinke the former) of walnuts." According to Evelyn he was
"an excellent droll," a " marveillous good-natured person,"
and "as to aspect beautifull." Once when challenged to a

the inability of ordinary folk to form any judgment on such matters.   During the four years that had nearly elapsed since he opposed Harrington's balloting schemes, his principles had apparently undergone no change, and he would have been the last man to submit his opinions to a consensus of popular prejudice.   On the contrary,—

"He showed finely whence it happens that good writers are not admired by the present age; because there are but few in any age who do mind anything that is abstruse and curious; . . . the generality of mankind pleasing themselves in the easy delights of the world, as eating, drinking, dancing, hunting, fencing, which we see the meanest men do best—that profess it.   A gentleman never dances so well as the dancing master; and an ordinary fiddler makes better music for a shilling than a gentleman will after spending forty."

Poor Pepys, himself "a gentleman fiddler," may have felt this last as a home thrust.   He seems to have recollected at this moment particular business of a pressing kind, and was off to Covent Garden, there "to buy a maske at the French house, Madame Charett's, for my wife."

So far from insisting that the majority of these places were really suited to learned or profound

duel he nominated "for the place a dark cellar, and the weapon to be a great carpenter's axe."   This turned the whole affair into ridicule, "and so it came to nought."

discussion, it has been rather my object to show that they provided a refuge for men of fashionable instincts—men who, like Pepys, were seeking to obtain something of the enjoyment and, it may be, frivolity, apart from the more harmful dissipations of polite society. Here both he and his friends could be temperate as they wished without going into exile for the purpose.

CHAPTER VII.

COFFEE HOUSES UNDER THE STUARTS: THE HOME OF LIBERTY.

"Coffee that makes the Politician wise,
  To see through all things with his half-closed eyes."
                                                    Pope.

IN this chapter we shall deal with the coffee house chiefly as a political institution which came into collision with the tyrannical government of the later Stuart kings: and for the sake of showing how continuous was that struggle, the chief events are here set down in chronological order.

Its general popularity had from the first suggested that our beverage might be made to
1660. yield a profitable addition to the revenue; accordingly, in the year of the Restoration, coffee was taxed *in a liquid state*, and orders were given that for every gallon sold should be paid by the makers thereof *fourpence*. It was afterwards further provided that none should keep open a coffee house, except such as had already given good security for

the payment of these dues, and had obtained a
Government licence, for which the sum of twelve-
pence must be paid : any one neglecting these regulations was liable to a fine of 5*l.* for every month
during which he continued the illegal sale.

The coffee houses seem to have been under close
surveillance by certain Government officials. One
of these was Muddiman, a good scholar and an
"arch rogue," who had formerly written for the
Parliament, and was now working in an underhand
manner as a paid spy. Another, whom Pepys
describes as Muddiman's successor, was the well-
known Roger l'Estrange.

L'Estrange's "Considerations and proposals
in order to the Regulation of the Press"
1663.
at once procured for him a post as its
"surveyor," with "the sole privilege of printing
and publishing all narratives, advertisements,
mercuries, intelligencers, diurnals, and other books
of public intelligence." In his *Intelligencer*,
commenced at the end of August, he notices with
alarm the ill-effects of "the ordinary written papers
of Parliament's news . . . making the coffee houses
and all the popular clubs judges of those councils
and deliberations which they have nothing to do
with at all."

Indeed, it was vain to hope for the extinction of liberty, so long as the number of printed libels was exceeded by the manuscript criticisms of which "the principall and professed dealers" were observed to be "some certain stationers and coffee-men," a great part of whose profit depended upon that "kinde of Trade;" accordingly we find it suggested "as a fair Expedient in this Case to insert a condition into the Licence of all Coffee-men not to transgresse."[1] Yet, owing to the Dutch war, which was at this time being waged, the Government seem to have been unwilling to proceed to extremes against these centres of disaffection: on the contrary, officials were specially anxious to pick up the coffee-house gossip; they observed carefully "what the Commonwealth man said, and what was replied for the Government;" they noted how the idea of a new ship to be called the *London*

[1] State Papers, Domestic Series, February 24th, 1662-3. For the former quotation, see Morley's "Sketch of English Literature," p. 710. L'Estrange was born in 1616, and educated at Cambridge. As a friend of Charles I. he barely escaped in the Civil War. He wrote several papers, e.g. the *City Mercury* and *Observator*, was consistent in politics, and was knighted by James II. For Muddiman's list of coffee houses, see Appendix. Sir John Birkenhead, in some sense Muddiman's successor, was among Harrington's opponents at the Rota.

was received by the assembled citizens, and how it was there reported that the systematic "selling of places makes men steal to raise their money."[1]

On the 22nd of June of the following year the great topic on the Exchange, and in a neighbouring coffee house, was the appearance of the enemy's fleet of sixty sail; but a timely success averted panic, and we learn (from the Diary, Aug. 1st) that the whole coffee house was "full of victory." Sometimes the war news supplied to the principal coffee houses was more punctual and more authentic than that which came through Government channels. The *Globe* may perhaps at this time have been in special favour with the authorities.[2] Upon occasion, too, these places were found to be convenient for the purpose of spreading news in

1664.

1665.

---

[1] A letter to Secretary Bennet, dated from "Coffee House," March 9th, 1664-5; see State Papers, Domestic Series, Record Office.

[2] In the *Intelligencer* for January 2nd, 1664-5, we read that no ships have "the benefit of the Present Peace with Algiers but such as carry with them a Pass from his Royal Highness the Duke of York . . . the said passes may be had at the office of Mr. Brigge at the Globe over against the North entrance of the Royal Exchange." For Token see Appendix.

favour of the Government: e.g. when Sir William
Batten, in a letter to his colleague, describes how
he has "sent to Captain Cook one of the Dutch
handcuffs prepared for our men; they have several
chains, and those engines are to go 100 on a
chain;" and, with a view to stirring up the warlike
instinct of the citizens, he desires Pepys to publish
this report "at the coffee houses, where it will
spread like leprosy." [1]

This half-hearted persecution did not prevent
even the poorer citizen from making the coffee
house his place of daily resort, and, in spite of all
attempts, the new institution continued to flourish,
until, as we have already seen, its growth was
temporarily checked by the twofold calamity which
overwhelmed the whole city.

One well-known coffee house remained un-
touched by the Fire, which raged from the Tower
to the Temple, and, in grateful memory of his
escape, James Farr issued a token wherein a rainbow is seen emerging from the clouds. On the
reverse of Farr's little medal was inscribed, " His
half-penny," so that we may include it amongst
the large number of copper and even leather coins

---

[1] Calendar of Admiralty State Papers, May 14th, 1665.

which were now being put forth by coffee-house keepers and others, with a view to business.

Without losing sight of our original purpose, we may see by a reference to the history of these trade tokens that the tyranny of the Stuart Government was equalled by their neglect of all that concerned the welfare of the mercantile classes. Yet the scarcity of "small change" dates back to the times of the Civil War, and is curiously illustrated by a "Declaration concerning Farthing Tokens," in which we learn that these were made by a Captain Knowles with "a quarter of an ounce of fine Pewter, that so we may not be cousened as from time to time we have been by Fathings of little worth."

Cromwell's Government seems to have made a vigorous attempt to obtain uniformity in this matter, and we read " of those that were taken about suspition of coyning false moneys," of the calling in of old farthing tokens, and of new ones issued at the office in Threadneedle Street.[1]

Evelyn was afterwards at no pains to conceal his disdain for "the Tokens which every Tavern

---

[1] See "A Perfect Diurnall," 1651, and "Mercurius Fumigosus," 1654. This subject is fully discussed by Burn in the introduction to his Catalogue of Traders' Tokens.

and Tippling-House (in the days of late Anarchy among us) presum'd to stamp and *utter for immediate Exchange,* as they were passable through the Neighbourhood, which, tho' seldom reaching farther than the next Street, or two, may happily in after times, come to exercise and busie the learned critic what they should signifie." [1] Yet the return of the Stuarts was so far from bringing relief, that, whilst the sovereign's dignity could not allow of his image being stamped upon any baser metal than silver, the poorer citizens no longer found their needs even partially supplied by a semi-official coinage.

From coins we can sometimes learn how far any particular Government was respected by the trading community of its day, and the aid of the numismatist is often required in settling an early Saxon or classical date; but, with all due deference to the lofty Evelyn, it may also be said that the study of these very tokens is a faithful, if humble, attendant upon that of History.

The fact that these "arrant trifles" were issued by the common people for the daily necessities of their still poorer neighbours, causes them to be

[1] "Numismata, a Discourse of Medals," p. 16 of ed. 1697 (1st edition, 1693).

of no mean value when the inquiry is concerning the habits, wants, and tastes of the average Englishman two hundred years ago. "Tokens," writes Mr. G. C. Williamson, "are essentially democratic;" they would never have been issued but for the indifference of the Government to a public need; and in them we have a remarkable instance of a people forcing a legislature to comply with demands at once reasonable and imperative. "Taken as a whole series," says the same authority, "they are homely and quaint, wanting in beauty, but not without a curious domestic art of their own." They usually bear on one side the name of the issuer, and on the other the place of issue; and in the field some device having reference to the trade, and upon the other side the issuer's initials, together sometimes with those of his wife.

A remarkable exception to the general simplicity is found in the coins belonging to one of the Exchange coffee houses. The dies of these tokens are such as to have suggested the skilled workmanship of John Roettier. The most ornate has the head of a Turkish Sultan at that time famed for his horrible deeds, ending in the tragedy of self-murder; its inscription runs,—

> " Morat ye great men did mee call ;
> Where Eare I came I conquer'd all."

Other interesting tokens are the leather ones issued from " Robins in Old Jewry," also from the Union and Chapter Coffee Houses. In reference to this kind of money [see illustration], the following lines of Davenant[1] are aptly quoted by Burn :—

> " Bury her gold with her !
> 'Tis strange her old shoes were not interr'd too
> For fear the days of Edgar should return,
> When they coin'd leather."

For a detailed account of these tokens the reader is referred to the catalogue in the Appendix, where they are given in full. The specimens preserved, and there are doubtless many unrepresented in these collections, show that the coffee houses of the Restoration were continually on the increase : many new ones were opened shortly after the Fire ; these showed a decided advance, being no longer limited to a single room up a flight of stairs, and in the matter of social and political importance they were destined far to outstrip former achievements.

---

[1] " The Wits " (act v., sc. 1). Played in 1633, printed in 1636. Sir William Davenant was at this time Poet Laureate. In his edition of 1853, Burn calls this a mere flourish and whimsy of the poet.

No. 5.

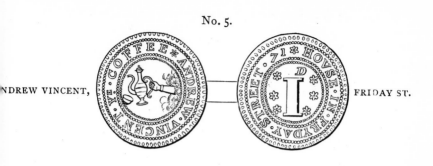

NDREW VINCENT,   FRIDAY ST.

No. 6.

ROBINS,   OLD JEWRY.

No. 7.

MARY LONG,   RUSSELL STREET.

No. 8.

CHAPTER COFFEE HOUSE,   PATERNOSTER ROW.

In the year 1667 Charles II. and the Duke of
1667. York were present at the acting of a play
called *Tarugo's Wiles*, or *The Coffee House*.
The piece opened in a lively manner, with a request on the part of its fashionable hero for a
change of clothes: accordingly Tarugo put off his
" Vest, hat, Perriwig, and sword," and served the
guests to coffee, whilst the apprentice acted his part
as a gentleman customer. Presently other "Customers of all Trades and Professions" came drop-
ping into the coffee house. These were not always
polite to the supposed coffee-man; one complained
of his coffee as being " nothing but warm water
boyl'd with burnt Beans," whilst another desired
him to bring "Chocolette that's prepar'd with
water, for I hate that which is encourag'd with
Eggs." The pedantry and nonsense uttered by a
" schollar " was perhaps an unfair specimen of
coffee-house talk; it is to be specially noticed
that none of the guests ventured upon politics.

In the end the coffee-master grew tired of his
clownish visitors, saying plainly, "This rudeness
becomes a suburb tavern rather than my coffee
house," and with the assistance of his servants he
"thrusts 'em all out of doors, after the schollars and
customers pay."

Turning with relief from what Pepys calls "the most ridiculous, insipid play that ever I saw in my life," we have in a broadside called " News from the Coffee House " an account of its "several sorts of Passions." Very different, and far from being tame or uninteresting to the authorities, is the style of conversation in this assembly. Here we find, with special mention of the "merchant 'prentice," the same mixture of company so characteristic of the early coffee houses :—

> " You that delight in wit and mirth,
>   And long to hear such news
> As comes from all parts of the earth,
>   Dutch, Danes, and Turks, and Jews,
> I'l send ye to a rendez vous,
>   Where it is smoking new ;
> Go hear it at a coffee house,
>   It cannot but be true.
>
> There battle and sea fights are fought,
>   And bloody plots display'd ;
> They know more things than ere was thought,
>   Or ever was betray'd.
> No money in the Minting-house
>   Is half so bright and new ;
> But coming from a coffee house,
>   It cannot but be true.
> Before the navies fell to work, they knew who should
>   be winner ;
>   They there can tell ye what the Turk
> Last Sunday had to dinner ;
>   Who last did cut Du Ruiter's corns,

. . . .

> There's nothing done in all the world,
>   From monarch to the mouse,
> But every day and night 'tis hurl'd
>   Into the coffee house.
>
> .   .   .   .
>
> A merchant 'prentice there shall show
>   You all and everything ;
> That has been done or is to do
>   'Twixt Holland and the king.
> What articles of peace will be,
>   He can precisely show ;
> What will be good for them or *wee,*
>   He perfectly doth know."

Doubtless the satire of this piece, printed " with allowance," was thought by the Government licenser to tell wholly against the absurd and extravagant conjectures eagerly welcomed as news by the citizens ; yet one of its prophecies came to have an unexpected, though partial, fulfilment in the appearance of the Dutch fleet upon the Thames. A coffee-house orator is actually made to declare that :—

> " Monsieur will cut our throats,
>   The French king will a girdle bring,
> Made of flat-bottom'd boats,
>   Shall compass England round about,
> Which must not be a few,
>   To give our Englishmen the Rout,
> This sounds as if 'twere true."

At all events, this unfortunate verse was omitted when the broadside was " reprinted and amended " in the year that England joined with France and again declared war on the Dutch.

When the noise of the foreign guns had ceased, then the strife of tongues broke out, and such was the freedom of speech that, in the words of a news-letter of the following month, " the scandal given to all sober, well-meaning men by coffee houses will, it is thought, give occasion for their inspection and the regulation of their abuses." [1]

For a time, however, the Government were so fully occupied with their project for ruling without a Parliament, and with negotiations for obtaining French aid, that they were content to abstain from any further attacks upon public liberty, and seem to have left the coffee houses pretty much to themselves.

We shall here describe Man's Coffee House, "the first near the Court." It forms a striking contrast to the ordinary resorts of the citizens, and may be taken as a fairly representative specimen of what, in later days, these places tended to become under the shadow and patronage of Royalty. Man, who was a Scotchman by birth, had followed General Monk to London, and

[1] Historical MS. Commission : the MSS. of S. H. Le Fleming, Esq., of Rydal Hall.

having set up a few years after the Fire in the neighbourhood of Whitehall, was "declar'd Coffee-Man to Charles II.," and until the palace was burned down his establishment was *facile princeps* amongst a number of lesser coffee houses.[1] The fashionable style of the company that resorted thither is curiously indicated by an advertisement in the *London Gazette* for the year 1674, offering a handsome reward to any one who can restore to the master of the Royal Coffee House a silver tobacco-box "with a Coat of arms on it, well engraven, being six escallop shells." At the time when "the London Spy" introduces us to this house, its eminent exclusiveness was a marked feature. Remoteness of situation, at the end of a long dark entry, favoured the notion of secrecy, and here it was that the "Black Guard of Quality," who carried the torches of great lords within, were indulging themselves in horse-play and in oaths as affected as the language in which

[1] Whitehall was partially burned in 1691, and again, except the banqueting-hall, in January, 1697-8. Man's business continued to flourish amid rivals. Mr. John Ashton, in his list of 500 coffee houses in the reign of Queen Anne, mentions Old Man's (at Charing Cross), Young Man's (opposite), New Man's, &c., in all six places bearing this name. Alexander Man was coffee-maker to William III.

they were uttered. We pass in with our guide,
who, afterwards a tavern-keeper, is neither friendly
nor impartial towards coffee-house customs;
though a probable acquaintance with the flunkies
below would make his admission more easy. As-
cending the stairs we enter what seems like "an
old-fashion'd Room of a Cathedral Tenement,"
where we find a lively scene, for the gaudy crowd
of beaus are "walking Backwards and Forwards
with their Hats in their Hands, not daring to convert 'em to their intended Use, lest it should put
the Foretops of their wigs into some Disorder."
"We squeezed through the Assembly," says Ned
Ward, "till we got to the end of the room," and
sitting down at a small table observed that,
"though there was abundance of Guests, there was
very little to do." In fact, these fashionable philosophers seem to have been more successful in
keeping undesirable company at a distance, than
in devising any serious occupation for themselves.

They neither smoked nor drank coffee, "for it
was as great a rarity to hear any Body call for a
Dish of Politician's Porridge, or any other Liquor,
as it is to hear a Spunger in a Company ask
what's to pay, or a Beau call for a Pipe of

Tobacco." Much time was passed in adjusting the curls of their perriwigs, and in exchanging "bows and cringes of the newest mode." Sometimes they stood with their hands in their pockets whispering about "new minuets," and suchlike important trifles ; or would resort to snuff-taking, and then "the clashing of their snush-box-lids, in opening and shutting, made more noise than their tongues ; and sounded as terrible in my Ears as the melancholy Tick of so many Death-watches."

Utterly regardless of frowns and "peevish wrinkles," Ned Ward, with his companions, procured "Instruments of Evaporation," insisted on smoking, and thereby cleared one corner of the room. Those whom he calls "the squeamish Tobacco-Haters" presently retired to the casements of the great window facing the street, when there came along a dumb man, who caused the mob to howl with delight, by artfully mimicking the beau "in the Strut, the Toss of the Wig, the carriage of the Hat, the Snush Box, the Fingering of the Foretop, the Hanging of the Sword."

There was indeed a mystery, about which the Spy could only make impertinent guesses, for "at the ends of this Principal Room were other Apartments, where, I suppose, the Beau-Politicks retired upon 'xtraordinary Occasions to talk Nonsense by themselves about State affairs." That the place was not without its importance in Ned Ward's time, appears from the lines which he professes to have " scribbled down in a Slate-Book " before departing :—

> " Here Persons who for Places wait,
>   Deceitful Courtiers Greet.
> And men of sense made Fools by Fate,
>   Their Crafty Patrons meet.
> Here Pension'd Spies like Saints appear,
>   Who do mens Hearts inspect
> And whisper in the Statesman's Ear,'
>   What they abroad collect.
>
> Here News by subtile Tongues is spread,
>   To try the listening crowd;
> But what is Truth's a secret made,
>   Whilst Lyes are Talk'd aloud.
> Beau Fools in Clusters here Resort,
>   And are so saucy grown,
> They'll ask my Lord, What News from Court?
>   Who smiles, and Answers none.
>
> To be inform'd few caring less ;
>   But ask as 'tis the Mode ;
> No knowledge seek, but how to Dress ;
>   Their Taylor is their god.
>
> .   .   .   .   .   .
>
> Both those who serve and Plague the State,
>   Do hither make their way ;
> And crowds of Humane vultures wait
>   To catch their silly Prey."

Doubtless when the crowds of would-be pensioners had taken to resort hither, and Government officials attended in order to meet their lesser employés, politics were only discussed with a great amount of deference for Court opinion. We have, however, a mention of Man's some twenty years earlier, which leads us to suppose that during the perplexities of "the merry monarch" these gay cavaliers were quite ready to adopt popular notions concerning "the Paapish Plaat."[1]

Returning to the story of the struggle for freedom, we find the Government at the beginning of the year 1672 preparing to strike a blow at the very existence of coffee houses. According to a news-letter, "the king, having been informed 1672. of the great inconveniences arising from the great number of persons that resort to coffee houses, has desired the Lord Keeper and

---

[1] It must be carefully noted that Ward's description was not published before 1698. In his "Compleat and Humorous Account of Clubs" the smokers in their turn are discomfited by having "the Parish engine turned upon them," and "wander about being a plague to various coffee houses—where they were unknown—after this manner they (i.e. the smokers) would clear a coffee house in half an hour, and all the time delight in it."

the Judges to give their opinion in writing how far he may lawfully proceed against them."[1]

The judges who were in town received an order to attend and advise the king upon this subject, in which his Majesty seems to have taken a keen personal interest. They were at first unable to come to a decision, for Sir William Jones, the Attorney-General, was "attached to the Faction," and was moreover unnerved by the ominous threat that "Mr. Attorney should answer for it in Parliament."

Being hard pressed for a reply, they gave such a halting judgment in favour of the king's policy as to remind us of the reluctant verdict wrung from the Arab doctors on a similar occasion (see Ch. II. p. 23). The English lawyers, in language which for its civility and indefiniteness would have been the envy of their Eastern brethren, declared that—

---

[1] Historical MS. Commission : MSS. of S. H. Le Fleming, Esq., February 19th, 1671-2. The judges seem to have been called together again after the issue of the first proclamation. The position of the coffee-men was more uncertain than that of innkeepers nowadays. " It was discovered that the statute made no mention of the time during which the licence should remain in force ; and from this omission a conclusion was drawn, that it must be considered revocable at pleasure " (Lingard, ix. p. 301).

" Retailing coffee *might* be an innocent Trade, as it *might* be exercised ; but as it is used at present, in the Nature of a common assembly, to discourse of Matters of State, News and *great Persons*, as they are Nurseries of Idleness and Pragmaticalness, and hinder the Expence of our native Provisions, they *might* be thought common nuisances."

According to Roger North, his own relatives deserve whatever credit may be connected with the closing of the coffee houses, and a suggestion that they should be summarily dealt with was made by a member of that family. The Hon. Dudley North (Commissioner of Customs to Charles II.), upon his return from Constantinople, related how in that city such were not suffered to exist, " it having been found that the People, by a Tendency to sedition, made an ill use of them." [1]

However, it is unlikely that Charles required the Sultan's example to incite him to what was in reality a favourite scheme : if he looked abroad at all, it was for French money and for French soldiers to assist in coercing his unruly people. As we shall presently see, Charles was probably waiting

[1] See " Life of Hon. Sir Dudley North," by Hon. Roger North. For preceding paragraph, see the " Examen," by Roger North, and his " Life of Francis North, Lord Keeper of the Great Seal under Charles II. and (as predecessor of Jeffreys) under James II."

to find a minister who should prove a fit instrument for his purposes.

As long ago as 1666 he had complained to the Lord Chancellor Clarendon of the freedom of speech that characterized these places, and of the evil reports concerning the Government which were circulated from thence throughout the country. Clarendon, who tells the story himself, strongly urged that the king should show to all men that coffee houses were not privileged places in the matter of libels. He suggested as an alternative that they should be wholly suppressed, or that spies should be present there to inform against those "who had talked with most licence in a subject that would bear complaint; upon which the proceedings might be in such a manner as would put an end to the confidence that was only mischievous in those meetings." The king professed to favour a combination of both expedients, and bidding Clarendon propose it that very day in council, "himself mentioned it with passion ;" he even directed that the Attorney-General should prepare a proclamation. With this opinion the Board seemed about to concur when, to the Chancellor's dismay, Sir William Coventry, who had shortly before been heard to inveigh against the permission of seditious prattling, now spoke earnestly upon the other side. His speech, like a piece of coffee-house oratory, was full of dark hints and innuendoes. The Government, said he, obtained from coffee a considerable revenue, and the king himself owed to these seemingly obnoxious places no small debt of gratitude in the matter of his own restoration ; for they had been permitted in Cromwell's time, and then " the King's friends had used more liberty of speech in those places than they durst do in any other." Moreover, it would be rash to issue a command so likely to be disobeyed ; better by far to remain content, " without running the hazard of ill being continued, notwithstanding his command to the contrary."

Charles' character has been a puzzle alike to contemporaries and to historians. Was he a mere loafer, with a mind wholly given up to Court trifles ? As such he was generally regarded by the outside public. Was he, as J. R. Green suggests, the most artful of plotters, whose serious countenance wore the mask of pleasure ? Did he care for nothing more than to be without care ? This, according to Hallam, explains his continuous longing to be irresponsible. In the scene before us we have the chief minister checkmated because he calculated his master too closely, and failed to allow enough for inconsistencies. It is not easy to say whether Charles was actually influenced by Sir William Coventry's arguments, or whether he was already planning to free himself from Clarendon's rather irksome control. At all events his Majesty pretended to be convinced, "and declined any further debate ; which put the Chancellor very much out of countenance, nor knew he how to behave himself."

Shortly after this Clarendon went into the banishment from which he was never to be recalled, and the *coup d'état*, so to speak, was not carried out until the year after that statesman's decease.

As might be expected in our country, this bold measure was not to be undertaken without an attempt to gain over popular opinion. 1673. In the "Grand Concern of England explained" we have, under the name of "several proposals offered to the consideration of Parliament," a somewhat lengthy statement of the Government policy. Indeed the closing of the coffee houses was only one out of many sweeping reforms herein suggested. A stop was to be put to further build-

ing in London, " the head being already too big
for the body; " country gentry were to be compelled to reside on their estates ; the excessive
wages of servants were to be reduced ; and the
multitude of stage coaches were to be prohibited
on the plea that " they effeminate his Majesty's
subjects." The same aristocratic instinct compels
this unknown " lover of his country " to object to
the London coffee houses as tending, after a still
more dangerous sort, to upset the social order :

"As for coffee, tea and chocolate, I know no good they
do; only the places where they are sold are convenient for
persons to meet in, sit half a day, and discourse with all
companies that come in of State matters, talking of news and
broaching of lies, arraigning the judgments and discretion
of their governors, censuring all their actions, and insinua-
ting into the ears of the people a prejudice against them ;
extolling and magnifying their own parts, knowledge and
wisdom, and decrying that of their rulers; which if suffered
too long, may prove pernicious and destructive."

After such a tirade we shall not be doing an
injustice to the writer by attributing his exaggeration to spitefulness :

"Very many of them," he declares, are devoted to the
worst of purposes and " are become scandalous for a man to
be seen in them ; which gentlemen not knowing do frequently fall into them by chance, and so their reputation is
drawn into question thereby."

The writer, who is evidently trying to make out

a case on behalf of authority, proceeds to argue
that the coffee houses

" Have undone many of the king's subjects, for they being
great enemies to diligence and industry, have been the ruin
of many serious and hopeful young gentlemen and tradesmen who . . . since these houses have been set up under
pretence of good husbandry, to avoid spending above one
penny or twopence at a time, have got to these coffee houses,
where, meeting friends, they have sat talking three or four
hours, after which a fresh acquaintance appearing, and so one
after another all day long, hath begotten fresh discourse, so
that frequently they have stayed five or six hours together
in one of them, all of which time their shops . . . their
business . . . their servants . . . their customers " have
been alike neglected !

In another pamphlet of this year we have a
similarly disdainful reference to the fresh notions
of economy and frugality, " he that comes often
saves 2*d*. a week in gazettes, and has his news and
his coffee for the same charge." It is likewise this
writer's intention to hold up to ridicule everything
connected with the popular, and in his eyes, vulgar
institution.[1] Yet even the caricaturist does not

[1] Very merry does he wax over the childish infirmities of
the poor coffee house waiter. This fellow was no traveller,
and yet spent his time in continued motion backwards and
forwards between the fireside and the table ; moreover his
tongue was lively and moved infinitely faster than his feet.
His thoughts were divided between the needs of his guests
and the question for ever upon their lips, viz. " What news

hint at anything of the nature of a conspiracy or democratic organization, the existence of which might have afforded a decent excuse for interference.

The only reply to this attack is somewhat wanting in vigour, and gives the impression that
1674-5. to reply at all was just now a task of considerable danger. It has a brief reference to the persecution by authority, and likens the adversary who, for the purpose of raking up scandal, had performed "a painful pilgrimage from one coffee house to another," to the equally dreaded exciseman reckoning the number of dishes.

At length the Government, with Danby as their

have you, master?" During the handing of the coffee cups he will get an answer ready and the thread of his political discourse is interrupted by such necessary parenthesis as, "Wife, sweep up those loose corns of tobacco, and see that the liquor boil not over." In whispered words he presently discloses to privileged guests secrets of state told him by one that is "barber to the taylor of a mighty great courtier's man." For this "Character of a coffee house with symptoms of a town wit, with allowance" [i.e. duly licensed] see ch. vi. 2, etc., also for "Coffee Houses Vindicated," of which Wood's copy (mentioned in "Life and Times of A. W.") is dated 1674. The reprint, "Harleian Miscellany," vol. vi. p. 465, is dated 1675, and may have been printed at the beginning of the year, or is a later edition, as it refers to a Royal Proclamation.

ruling spirit, resolve upon prompt and vigorous action ; these seminaries of sedition are to be closed at once and closed for ever. The following is a copy of the proclamation whose heading announces the contents with exactness :

BY THE KING. A PROCLAMATION FOR THE SUPPRESSION OF COFFEE HOUSES.

Charles R.

Whereas it is most apparent that the multitude of Coffee Houses of late years set up and kept within this kingdom, the dominion of Wales, and town of Berwick-upon-Tweed, and the great resort of Idle and disaffected persons to them, have produced very evil and dangerous effects ; as well for that many tradesmen and others, do herein mispend much of their time, which might and probably would be employed in and about their Lawful Calling and Affairs ; but also, for that in such houses . . . divers false, malitious and scandalous reports are devised and spread abroad to the Defamation of his Majestie's Government, and to the Disturbance of the Peace and Quiet of the Realm; his Majesty hath thought fit and necessary, that the said Coffee Houses be (for the future) Put down, and suppressed, and doth . . . strictly charge and command all manner of persons, That they or any of them do not presume from and after the Tenth Day of January next ensuing, to keep any Public Coffee House, or to utter or sell by retail, in his, her or their house or houses (to be spent or consumed within the same) any Coffee, Chocolet, Sherbett or Tea, as they will answer the contrary at their utmost perils . . . [all licenses to be revoked].

Given at our Court at Whitehall, this third-and-twentieth day of Dec. 1675 in the seven-and-twentieth year of our Reign.

SMALLCAPS GOD SAVE THE KING.

It is not a usual thing for a proclamation put forth on the 29th day of one month to be recalled on the 8th day of the next; yet such was the feeling aroused that eleven days fully sufficed for this unfortunate experiment; it is said that men of all parties cried out when they experienced the loss of their accustomed haunts, or, as Sir Roger North reluctantly allows in his Examen, "a convulsion and discontent would unavoidably follow: And that, I believe, was the real cause the proclamation was so soon withdrawn."

To retreat in time was quite in accordance with the policy of a king who, notwithstanding all his rashness, had determined "never to set out on his travels again;" to do so gracefully and without an appearance of compulsion was by no means an easy matter. The fact that the Government had not been slow to blazon abroad their own success now increased the difficulty.[1]

1676.

Yet even this delicate task was fully accomplished by the "additional proclamation concerning coffee

---

[1] In a newsletter of January 4th country folk are informed that "the most seditious, indecent, scandalous discourses of these places" had "at last produced this proclamation for suppressing them." Historical MS. Commission.—MSS. of Le Fleming, Esq.

houses," which announced that, subject to some few restrictions, these places would be allowed to continue as before. The king had, in the meantime, received a petition from divers of the coffee house keepers concerning their grievances ; and so we read that " His Majesty, out of his princely consideration, out of his royal compassion," and in return for humble confession of former miscarriages and abuses committed, and on condition of taking the oaths of allegiance and supremacy and of entering into recognizances to the extent of 500*l.*, " doth declare his royal pleasure to be, that all and every of the retailers of the liquors aforesaid " shall be allowed to keep open " until the four-and-twentieth day of June next." The Government do not seem to have had the faintest intention of again closing these houses in any month of any year. This date was evidently mentioned for the sake of appearances. It should also be noticed that on the 7th day of January a proclamation had been issued " for the better discovery of seditious libellers," which answered a two-fold purpose ; it made an excellent show of following up the first severity, and, when the time came to retire enabled the Government to do so with their faces towards the enemy. Thus it was made to appear that the real end in view was the capture of seditious personages who had, unfortunately for the coffee houses, taken to resort thither. Lastly, it would seem that the formidable sum of 500*l.* was not after all to be demanded from these poor keepers of refreshment bars, if only they would be considerate enough to assist the objects of the Government by doing their best to exclude from the coffee house premises these much dreaded libels.

Upon this matter of Government interference and successful popular resistance, I have not dwelt at greater length than its importance seemed to justify. The contest was concerning essentials. A battle for freedom of speech was fought and won over this question at a time when Parliaments were infrequent and when the liberty of the Press did not exist.[1]

[1] Historians have devoted considerable attention to the subject. In this essential matter of proclamations—as Hallam styles it—the Government of Charles II. was more cautious than his father's, and strove hard to effect its measures without openly violating the constitution. Roger North, whose Examen through thick and thin defends the Stuart policy, is angry at Kennet's assertion (" Complete History of England. . . writ by a learnet and Impartial Hand") that the coffee houses were closed because the people of England were so "jealous of Popery and the French power." That jealousy, as we now know, was not entertained without

It was not long before a political crisis revealed the importance of this victory. Shaftesbury 1677. having given his enemies an undoubted advantage by declaring the continual prorogation of parliament to be equivalent to a dissolution, was at once thrown into prison, there to remain until he had craved for pardon upon his bended knee. Yet the Government success was marred by the boldness of the citizens in asserting their opinion. "The attempt," said North, "to send the four lords to the Tower availed nothing, for the coffee houses still maintained the point," and he adds that none dare venture in them unless able to argue the question whether the Parliament were dissolved or not.

The impression derived from our next view of coffee house proceedings is not distinctly favourable. Had it been possible, during the time when the Popish scare was at its height, to issue an edict for their suppression, this might have cured the

good reason. Even Hume, who regards the incident as in itself trivial, admits that it "tends strongly to mark the genius of the English Government, and of Charles' administration during this period." Lingard (vol. ix. p. 301) says, "It gave a real foundation to charges which before rested merely on conjecture . . . an unanswerable proof of the arbitrary projects secretly cherished by the Court."

madness of the people and so have been the means of saving many innocent lives.[1]

The air was thick with intrigue, and there were many like Dangerfield who, upon his own confession, was getting up a sham plot in order to gain by the credulity of Papists or of anti-Papist fanatics. Of "the Major," an old officer in the Parliamentary army, we learn that he frequented the coffee house and that "he spoke well, with art and with authority that touch'd men's hearts, and was not unprovided with those that touched their interests," being "willingly heard and much applauded." Yet, his knowledge of human nature notwithstanding, this hero and orator was so completely taken in by Dangerfield as to contribute towards the funds needed for his elaborate pre-

---

[1] The proposal actually occurs amongst "eight things offered to the consideration of the king, lords and commons" (in a quaint tract called "The Present Great Interest, both of King and People," dated Sept. 16th, 1679) "that the nurseries of sedition and rebellion (i.e. the coffee houses) be forthwith put down, and some reasonable compensation given to the persons of that profession, who shall suffer thereby." In this tract Shaftesbury is probably alluded to as "the old cunning statesman" who stirs· up discontent and lets forth doubtful intelligence at each coffee house, that it may look two ways and neither of them true nor understood."

parations.[1] At first Dangerfield's plan seems to have been to inform against the Presbyterians. He tells how by frequenting the coffee houses he "came to a knowledge of the times and discovered them to be much inclined to sedition, speech therein was very free and treason was spoken with that liberty as though there were no laws against it." He also mentions a challenge left "at the coffee house to have thirty men or upwards, ready armed with trunchions, pistols, poynards, etc."

In his narrative of "the design to charge those of the Presbyterian party with a pretended conspiracy," we are furnished with a list of the principal and "most factious" of the coffee houses supposed to have been visited by his agents.

First on the catalogue stands "Farr's coffee house, the Rainbow near the Temple," and it is interesting to note that "Sir Henry Blunt" is now mentioned in the same connection as a frequenter of clubs ; it is certain that the worthy knight had not given up his fondness for coffee houses, as

This account of the Major is quoted from Tait's *Edin. Magazine*, (n.s. 22 : 104), as also the following quotation and that from North (on p. 177) concerning King's evidence. This interesting article on "Coffee Houses of the Restoration," though not strictly limited to the period suggested by its title, has proved very helpful.

Aubrey, writing at this time, says that he was in the habit of attending John's in Fuller's Rents. Farr's coffee house, its original proprietor being still alive, was visited by Dangerfield every night, until " a quarrel " took place, i.e. perhaps until he was ejected upon suspicion of being a dishonourable spy.

Proctor's or Procter's stands second. In one of the many " narratives of the late design," the author says, " being at Mr. Proctor's coffee house at Charing Cross I there met with a paper entitled Discovery of the Plot." Perhaps this was one of the " base pamphlets " written by Nevill, and sent, according to Dangerfield's own account, " sealed up in papers to Man's coffee house, to Farr's and to Proctor's, and others."

Man's at Charing Cross comes third on the list. We have also mention of Garraway's and Jonathan's near the Old [i.e. Royal] Exchange, Forde's in Essex Buildings, and Combe's in Bartholomew Lane. There were " divers others "; a reputed priest " frequented the coffee houses for the same end that I did ; and I sent to little petty coffee houses about the town." The information thus obtained was taken to headquarters by Dangerfield, who went up to Lord Powis " and had much dis-

course about opinions I met with in coffee houses,
and received instructions that I should . . . find out
some idle persons that appeared well in apparel,
and give them money to go to the coffee houses."
The end in view was not to discover or to form a
real plot, but to bring it about that "the coffee
houses might ring of the general apprehension of
some notorious villainies ready to break forth from
the Presbyterian party."

The clubs, taverns and coffee houses seem to
have been at this time alike emancipated from
control. Into the last named newspapers were
brought "wet from the press." Their eager guests
are described as tossing the *Gazettes* and *Intelligencers* up and down, and that "with a certain
frankness of conversation, agreeable to a people
that abhor starch and pedantry." The writer who
speaks thus warns against the mischief of rearing
"a massive structure" upon so slight a foundation
as evidence derived from coffee houses and taverns.
He might have gone further, and have said that
without any foundation whatever the most palpable
falsehoods were sometimes believed in these places.
Here is a sufficiently quaint production which
relates to our friend Samuel Pepys (the name
being often spelt and still pronounced as given

below) who was at this time in serious danger on account of his supposed Romanist doings. It occurs, without date, amongst Pepys' MSS. and is, together with the newspaper references, here quoted from the Appendix to Lord Braybrooke's edition of the Diary.

[Endorsed—"The Coffee House Paper, wherein ye scandalous intelligence touching Mr. Pepys."]

On Tuesday last, Mr. Peeps went to Windsor, having ye confidence yt he might kisse ye king's hand ; and being at Court, mett the Lord Chamberlain and made his complent to his Lordshipp. But his Lordshipp told him yt he wondered he should presume to come to Court before he had cleared himselfe, being charged with treason ; whose answer was, his innocency was such, that he valued not anything he was charged with ; soe parted from his Lordshipp ; but by the favour of some courtiers, he was brought into ye king's presence ; but so soon as his Majestie saw him he frowned and turned aside, showing his dislike of seeing him there."

This delightfully detailed statement, as it related to a somewhat prominent official, was gravely contradicted in the following terms :

" These are to give notice that all and every part of the relation published in the *Domestic Intelligencer* the 9th of this instant September, is as to the matter, and every particular therein mentioned, altogether false and scandalous, there having no such passage happened, nor anything that might give occasion to that report."

During the period of reaction that followed upon this excitement coffee houses were not so prominent; though an Exchange Alley Dialogue of 1681 tells how these places, except Garraway's, were "most, if not all, *Whiggified* hereabouts": their favourite neighbourhood was not forgotten when, in 1682, the Court of Common Council issued a proclamation against book hawkers, by whom "Cornhill and passages about the Royal Exchange, and coffee houses" were "much pestered." [1]

[1] At the great Fair held on the Thames during the Frost of the following year (middle of December, 1683 to February, 8), were to be seen "the first Tavern built on Freezeland-street," and the Duke's Coffee House [N.B. The well-known "Floating Coffee House" was of later date]. Our Illustration is reproduced from a Broadside entitled Wonders on the Deep; OR, The most exact Description of the Frozen RIVER of THAMES. . . . Explanation of the Piece in Figures. Figure 1. The Temple-Stairs. 2. The Duke of York's Coffee House. 3. The Tory-Booth. 4. The Booth with the Phœnix Insur'd. 5. The Roast-Beef-House. 6. The Half-way-House. 7. The Bare-Garden Booth. 8. The Musick-House Booth. 9. The PRINTER'S Booth. 10. The Raffling-Booth. 11. The Horn-Tavern. 12. The Temple-Garden, where people lookt on Frost-Fair. 13. The Barge drawn with a Horse. 14. The Drum-Boat. 15. The Boat drawn on Wheels by Men. 16. The Bull Bated. 17. The Dutch Chear sliding round. 18. The Boys Sliding. 19. Playing at Nine-pins. 20. Men Sliding with Sckates. 21. The Sledges of Coles. 22. A Booth. 23. Boys climbing the Trees in the Temple to see the Bull-Bating. 24. The Toy-shops. 25. London Bridge. 26. The six Tinkers. 27. The Foot-ball Play. 28. The Coach with three Wheels, mov'd by Clock-work. 29. The common Hackney-Coaches.

FAIR ON THE THAMES, 1683.

After a time dark but not untruthful rumours concerning the dealings of the English with the French Court began to circulate in coffee houses. When, however, King James was firmly seated on the throne their Puritan frequenters had something even more practical to discuss; here it was that " King's evidence were biggest with awful hints of the next batch of victims to come before Judge Jeffries."

1685-8.

This mention of the still dreadful name brings us to the final stage of the Stuart persecution, which was to end with the overthrow of that dynasty. As in the days of power and insolence Jeffreys found no topic unsuited for his ridicule, we need not be surprised that the coffee houses came in for at least one satirical allusion. On the occasion of his trying Compton, Bishop of London, before the Court of High Commission, that prelate, as Campbell relates in his " Lives of the Lord Chancellors," complained of having no copy of the indictment. Jeffreys replied to this excuse that "all the coffee houses had it for a penny." The case being resumed after the lapse of a week, the

30. The throwing at the Cock. 31. The Ox Roasting over against Whitehall. 32. The Man riding on the Thames. 33. Hot Gingerbread. 34. The Hunting of the Fox. 35. Knives or Combs.

Bishop again protested that he was unprepared, owing to his continued difficulty in obtaining a copy of the necessary document. Jeffreys was obliged once more to adjourn the case, and in so doing offered his bantering apology :

" My lord," said he, " in telling you our commission was to be seen in every coffee house I did not speak with any design to reflect on your lordship, as if you were a haunter of coffee houses. I abhor the thoughts of it ! "

As the judge had once been distinctly opposed to the party and the principles which he went to such a length in supporting, so had he formerly owed something to the very institution against which his last blow was directed. Roger North relates (and Campbell repeats the story) that :

" After he was called to the bar he used to sit in coffee houses and order his man to come and tell him that company attended him at his chamber ; at which he would huff and say, ' let them stay a little, I will come presently,' and thus made a show of business." [1]

---

[1] In the " Life of Jn. Radcliffe M.D.," it is related that Dr. Hanne's footman was ordered to feign similar requests. On one occasion this fellow entering Garraway's, at the time when the coffee house was fullest, demanded of the company whether his master was present, as several lords had need of his immediate attendance. Radcliffe took him up with the dry rebuke : " No, no, friend, you are mistaken, the Doctor wants those Lords."

There is no need to blacken the character of Jeffreys by pressing this particular charge of ingratitude, nor must we attribute his final measure to any settled design of tyranny; it was evidently a last resource, and only intended to keep the good people of England in ignorance of the preparations made for their deliverance. The same news-letter (Historical MS. Commission, Le Fleming, No. 3276), which tells how "last night Dr. Hough and the other fellows of Magdalen Coll., Oxford, were restored," reports an order "that no Coffee or publique house do keep any written or any other news save ye Gazett," and that in a personal interview the Lord Chancellor told the Justices of Middlesex and Westminster:

"They must take care herein to punish offenders, and not to suffer any p. son w^hsoever to talke of State affaires."[1]

A similar letter by an unknown writer is preserved in the "Ellis Correspondence," and is addressed to a Government official of that name resident in Ireland. The editor comments on this strange proceeding of Jeffreys and his master "at a moment

[1] Through the kindness of Mr. S. H. le Fleming and of the Provost of Queen's College, this quotation has been verified from the original MS. at Queen's Coll., Oxford.

when they were anxious to become popular, and when it was peculiarly important for them to show respect for the liberties of the subject." It is written on the very same day, viz. the 9th of October, and commences by saying, " We are still in the dark in great measure as to the Dutch fleet, our last Holland letters being of the 28th past." In almost identical language the action of Jeffreys is related. This document indeed forms a fitting close to the chapter, for it is more emphatic than the former, when it records that he,

"by the king's command, directed the Justices of Peace of Middlesex to suppress all coffee houses and other public houses that deal in newsletters, or expose to the public any foreign or domestic newspapers besides the printed Reports."

180 / NEW BY STEP DEGREE

CHAPTER VIII.

DEVELOPMENT AND DECLINE.

Where loyalists brew there fanaticks bake too
And the good will be mixt with the evil.
Coffee Scuffle, 1662.

THE many-sided development of coffee house life makes it needful to touch upon several matters which, so far as details are concerned, belong strictly to a later period. Though a complete record of such an establishment as Lloyd's with its world-wide " News " would bring us right down to our own times of steamboat and electricity, yet we will speak a few words about the commercial aspect of our subject. According to Mr. Frederick Martin, the establishment of coffee houses exercised a great influence upon the business of marine insurance ; they " proved very convenient meeting places for men engaged in a common object not requiring much time, and were as if made for underwriters." The original Lloyd set up in Tower Street, where he is first heard of shortly before the

Revolution.   Though this locality was well suited for a business connected with shipping, he moved after about four years to the corner of Abchurch Lane, Lombard Street, and was now " in the very centre of the mercantile life of the period."   In another four years was commenced, with a view to shipping and mercantile affairs, his famous " News ": and again at the end of another such period, i.e. in the year 1700, we find that " The Wealthy Shop-keeper " was wont to resort thither as to a recog-nized centre of business :

> Then to Lloyd's Coffee House he never fails,
> To read the letters and attend the sales.

Hain's, as early as 1675, and John's, just after the Revolution, both these coffee-houses being in Birchin Lane, were marts of some importance. Shipping sales were held in the latter until the superior arrangements of Lloyd's attracted trade thither.   Though " John " had set up in the neigh-bourhood of the Exchange before his enterprising rival, there is nothing to identify him with the person of the same name and trade in Holborn, or with the still earlier mention in the ballad of 1665, where we have " John's admir'd curled pate " as a coffee house sign.

Garraway's chief fame as a commercial resort

belongs to the 18th century, and yet as early as 1673 we read of "a standing lottery of books" to be disposed of in this place; and at the same date sales of wine were held here "by the candle."[1]

Their part in the long and successful struggle for liberty proved at last that the coffee houses had become naturalized as an English institution; yet objectors were slow to forget that coffee was the product of a foreign soil, and did in no way

---

[1] I.e. by auction, while an inch of candle burns. For the situation of the chief coffee houses near the Exchange, see map. In chap. vi. (pp. 117, 130) the reader will find an early account of these places as business haunts and "nurseries of temperance." It is worth mentioning as a proof that the coffee houses did not come suddenly into the confidence of business men, that "The Little London Directory" of 1677 (reprinted in 1863) seems to be without a reference to any who left an address there according to a custom which, at Garraway's, dates from 1683.

Mr. Martin, from whose valuable History of Lloyd's I have taken my account of that coffee house, quotes from No. 61, etc., of "Lloyd's News" the following announcement: "All gentlemen, merchants, or others, who are desirous to have this News in a whole Sheet of Paper [two leaves instead of one leaf] for to write their own private Concerns in, or other intelligence for the Countrey, may be supply'd with them, done upon very good paper, for a penny a sheet at Lloyd's Coffee House in Lombard Street." This practice was not unknown in the case of newspapers of several years later. Lloyd discontinued his paper for a number of years, and only re-started it in 1726 as "Lloyd's List."

tend to "the encouragement of native drunkenness," or, as North has it, "we contemn our own
excellent and more wholesome drinks ... and as
if the English could affect everything because it is
Foreign, we have also a new chargeable importation of coffee, which of all others seems to be most
useless, since it serves neither for nourishment nor
debauchery." Such testimony reminds us that
even down to the end of Charles II.'s reign coffee
was looked upon rather as a new check upon
license than as an added luxury. From a business
point of view this quotation is noteworthy, for it
occurs amongst instances given of the decay of our
importations, and it is clear that a constant dread
of this *chargeable importation* had full weight with
writers whose notion of political economy was well
expressed by the author of "The Grand Concern,"
when he said "trade is a great mystery." Even
after the Revolution we find London merchants
obliged to petition the House of Lords against
new import duties on coffee, and it was not until
the year 1692 that Government "for the greater
encouragement and advancement of trade, and the
greater importation of the said respective goods
or merchandises," discharged one half of the
obnoxious tariff.

This partial and, as it proved, temporary change of policy is to be accounted for by the fact that those dues, when really enforced, proved so excessive as to bring the trade to a standstill, and reduce the revenue therefrom to a mere trifle.[1] Still more convincing was the discovery that the berry might be looked upon as an export and be forwarded to the Colonies. As Houghton says, when discussing "the political uses of coffee," doubtless the gain of what is sent abroad would pay the first cost of all that is spent at home, and, from a theoretical point of view, "one of the best ways to make advantage of Foreign Trade is to use such wares much at home, and that will teach all we trade with to follow our example. It does thus in silks, callicoes, pepper, tobacco, and several other things." If our worthy author expected the citizens of London to order the manner of their drinking, smoking and dress with a special view to colonial imitation, he was making a great demand upon their public spirit; and he seems more practical when he tells how coffee has " in-

---

[1] The duty was no longer to be paid at the coffee houses upon demand of an officer, but handed in at the Custom House. See for the petition, " Report of House of Lords MSS., 1689," and D. Pickering for the Law of 1692.

creased the trade of tobaccos and pipes, earthen dishes, tin wares, newspapers, coals, candles, sugar, tea, chocolate, and what not!"

Of the colonial trade little need be said here; it was still in its infancy when the troubles of the Revolution occurred: only 510 cwt. of coffee had been registered for exportation in the previous year, and even this small amount was now diminished. However, there is mention of a "London coffee house" in Boston, at which books were sold, as early as 1689. When once they obtained a start in America the coffee houses speedily became popular; with this difference, that they were generally the meeting places of those who were conservative in their views regarding the church and the state; being friends of the ruling administration, such persons were termed "Courtiers" by their adversaries the Dissenters and Republicans.[1]

Our authority calculates the yearly sale of coffee at about 70 tons for England alone (100 for the United Kingdom), making out the expenditure to be some £20,000, and treble that amount "if it

[1] One was started at New York in 1701. See "Old New York Coffee Houses," *Harper's Monthly*, March, 1882. I have referred to Drake's "History of Boston" for the statement about the Coffee House in that city, but have not been able to light upon the passage.

were to be all sold in coffee houses." He also reckons that the average Englishman did not drink quite half a pint of coffee in the year, though some two years later, correcting this statement originally made in 1699, he tells how the cheapness of coffee had increased its use by something like one half, and adds that there were probably few trades in London employing more houses and paying greater rents.

If we could trust to statistics loosely quoted in round numbers, it would be clear that the London coffee houses towards the close of the 17th century were even more numerous than at a later period. Du Four, the French historian of coffee, writing as early as 1683, declares upon the information, as he says, of several persons who had stayed in London, that there are in this city alone more than 3000 of these places (ils vont au dela de trois mille), and the statement is repeated in 1687 by M. de Blegny in his " Bon Usage du Caffé." Hatton's remark (in the " New View of London ") that there were "near 3000 " in 1708 is sometimes, though wrongly, set down as a misprint for 2000, which last is said to be the official reckoning of the number before the year 1715.

We may here add something to what has

already been said concerning the literary bearings of our subject.   Yet it would be easier to enlarge upon the business aspect of the coffee houses than to set before the reader a satisfactory account of their attainments from an intellectual point of view. In this latter attempt we are entirely without the help of figures; and, were it possible to give a sort of census of the "geniuses" who from time to time brightened these places by their presence, a bare enumeration would be sufficiently tantalizing.

Even when we confine our inquiries to a single instance, and endeavour to do justice to the renown of a coffee house of which the name is most familiar, we are met by one serious difficulty— the fame of Will's had in some measure passed away before it became a custom to record conversation upon literary topics.   Moreover a contemporary source which has hitherto been so helpful now fails us almost entirely.   Perhaps the most provoking entry in the whole of Pepys' Diary is that which tells how, on the evening of the 3rd of February, 1663-4, he just looked in, on his way home from Covent Garden, "at the great coffee house there, where I never was before: where Dryden the poet, I knew at Cambridge, and all the wits of the town, were assembled." With this glimpse Pepys turns away, nor does he give us any further particulars as to Dryden and his brilliant coterie.[1]

The silence of Pepys is not the less to be regretted since, in judging of his conversation, Dryden's contemporaries express very different opinions. Congreve, who knew him intimately, speaks of his being easy of access but unwilling to intrude, and, whilst ready to communicate his knowledge, entirely without taint of pedantry. Dryden freely admits the want of fluency with which his enemies taxed him, yet Johnson explains his reticence as due to the pride of conscious ability. Though we are told that he was gentle enough in offering hints to authors and in accepting criticisms on his own composition, yet the autocrat of the " Literary Club " feels it necessary to defend his predecessor for " magisterially presiding over the younger writers, and assuming the distribution of literary fame." One fact is

---

[1] On that night were present also " Harris the player, and Mr. Hoole of our College ;" Pepys adds, as if regretfully : " And if I had time then, or could at other times, it will be good coming thither, for there, I perceive, is very witty and pleasant discourse. But I could not tarry, and, as it was late, they were all ready to go away."

See p. 137 for Pepys' report of a coffee house talk upon literary topics by Sir William Petty.

clear, namely, that Dryden sat night after night at Will's, discussing poetry and kindred topics with all comers, and there presided just as Ben Jonson had formerly reigned in the Mitre Tavern, and as Addison in later times held sway at Button's coffee house.[1]

In order to realize this scene it is necessary to have recourse to out-of-the-way sources, for even in Johnson's day tradition retained little concerning Dryden's habits and amusements :

[1] Opinion was not yet settled as to whether the realm of literature should be regarded as a Republic or an Elective monarchy. Dr. Johnson, who deemed a tavern chair to be the throne of human felicity, punningly refused the title of Dictator when applied to him at the Club, and Boswell quaintly likens his hero to the Cham of Tartary, whilst Goldsmith vehemently protested against such despotism within the commonwealth of letters ; similarly the envious Pope complained of Addison's being unable to endure "a rival near the throne." Dryden, indeed, imagined a dynasty of dulness, and allowed his adversary to wield Jove's sceptre and his thunderbolt, willingly owning him " without dispute, through all the realms of nonsense absolute." A biographer would here change the word "nonsense" into "English," and so transfer the honours from this "Pretender" to one who was a Prince of Poets. Lastly, a contemporary critic speaks of Dryden as "an abdicated Prince," who leaves Congreve "successor of his throne :" "Congreve is the poetic Prince of Wales, not at St. Germains, but at Will's his Court." (An Epistle to Blackmore, quoted by Scott ; Life of Dryden, p. 369.)

"Of the only two men whom I have found to whom he was personally known," says the Doctor, "one told me that at the house which he frequented, called Will's Coffee House, the appeal upon any literary dispute was made to him ; and the other related that his armed chair, which in the winter had a settled and prescriptive place by the fire, was in the summer placed in the balcony, and that he called the two places his winter and his summer seat. This is all the intelligence which his two survivors afforded me."

Nor could Boswell's diligent inquiries elicit much further information from the Doctor. Yet to the very close of his life Dryden was regular at Will's, and, as Malone informs us, so early as 1674, it was observed that he had already been a frequenter of the Covent Garden coffee house for fourteen years. Johnson also alludes to the fact that the poet was "prais'd and beaten for another's rhymes," i.e. on account of some satirical verses which reflected upon the king, and gave dire offence to the Earl of Rochester and other exalted personages. The lord in question, whose own verses the muse was "fond to inspire and ashamed to avow," hired a ruffian with a cudgel and exulted in his supposed revenge. Here is a contemporary reference to this outrage, which shows that it was both cruel and unprovoked :

"On Thursday last Mr. Dryden, the poet, coming from the coffee house in Covent Garden, was set upon by three or four fellows, and very sorely beaten, but likewise very much cutt and wounded with a sword. It is imagin'd that this has happened to him because of a late satyr that is laid at his door, tho' he positively disowned it."

This took place in the year 1679 when, as we have already seen, the nation was gone temporarily mad about plots and libels and unfounded accusations of all kinds. Another anecdote, also witnessed to by contemporary evidence, shows that within the coffee house itself, Dryden, having adopted the religion as well as the political cause of the Stuart dynasty, laid himself open to attacks less violent but scarcely less galling. The Bishop of Carlisle, in writing on January 27, 1686-7, from the Rose Tavern, states that the new Warden of All Souls, Oxford, is to be a Mr. Finch, the son of the Earl of Winchelsea, and " an ingenious young gentleman," who lately meeting Dryden in a coffee house in London, publicly before all the company wished him much joy of his *new* religion :

" Sir," said Dryden, " you are very much mistaken ; my religion is the *old* religion." " Nay," replied the other, " whatever it be in itself I am sure 'tis new to you."

The force of this remark was weakened and its impertinence increased by the added taunt :

" for within these few days you had no religion at all." [1]

---

[1] Historical MSS. Commission, MSS. of le Fleming,

Another incident concerning Dryden at Will's shows that the poet was not invulnerable even within his own domain of poetry and criticism. He had in MacFlecknoe triumphantly distinguished between his opponents, for " the rest to some faint meaning make pretence, but Shadwell never deviates into sense." His success, however, led him, according to the egotistic account of his youthful critic, to boast incautiously.

" I was about seventeen when I first came up to town," says Dean Lockier, " an odd-looking boy, with short rough hair, and that sort of awkwardness which one always brings up at first out of the country with one. However, in spite of my bashfulness and appearance, I used, now and then, to thrust myself into Will's. . . . The second time that ever I was there, Mr. Dryden was speaking of his own things, as he frequently did, especially of such as had been lately published. ' If anything of mine is good,' says he, ' 'tis MacFlecnoe ; and I value myself the more upon it, because it is the first piece of ridicule written in heroics.' "

The bashful youth plucked up courage to say that it was a fine poem " but not the first that was ever writ that way." Upon this Dryden turned to him sharply with the question, " How long have you been a dealer in poetry?" When the critic persisted, and mentioned authors from whom

Esq., January 27, 1686-7. See for the former quotation Dec. 23, 1679.

several "strokes" had been borrowed, the poet replied, "'Tis true, I had forgot them." Dryden, whose haste sometimes allowed him to take from others what he had not time to acknowledge, received the rebuke good-naturedly, deigning to honour the youth with a special invitation; "and," says Dean Lockier, "I was well acquainted with him after, as long as he lived." [1] The well-known parody by Montagu and Prior touches upon this weakness and affords us a curious view of the company who daily assembled at Will's to receive in all humility the instructions of their chief:

> "I've heard much talk of the Wits' coffee house,
> Thither, says Brindle, thou shalt go and see
> Priests sipping coffee, Sparks and Poets tea;
> Here rugged Frieze, there Quality well drest,
> These baffling the Grand-Seigniour, those the Test.

> .   .   .   .   .   .

[1] MacFlecknoe was published in 1682, and Francis Lockier, afterwards Dean of Peterborough, was born in 1668. See "Anecdotes of Books and Men," by the Rev. Joseph Spence, 1820. This first conversation with Dryden took place in the year 1685, when he was of two years' standing in the University. Lockier caused his MSS. containing this and other interesting anecdotes to be burned. Buckingham's "Rehearsal'" (p. 3, 5th ed., 1687) rather absurdly represents Dryden as confessing that he frequented "a coffee house, or some other place where witty men resort," in order to practise the arts of a plagiarist.

But above all . . .
Is the poetic Judge of Sacred Wit,
Who does i' the darkness of his glory sit.
And as the Moon who first receives the light,
With which she makes these Nether Regions bright ;
So does he shine, reflecting from afar,
The Rayes he borrow'd from a better Star.
For rules which from Corneille and Rapin flow,
Admir'd by all the scribbling herd below,
While he does dispense unerring truths.
'Tis schism, . . . offence
To question his, or trust your private sense."

Dryden had in turn his satellites who, to continue somewhat freely the above illustration, revolved at various distances around their great luminary. The best known of these was named Julian the rhymester, a drunken but witty fellow, who obtained a living chiefly by transcribing lampoons and multiplying copies according to demand.[1] In another passage of the " Hind and Panther transvers'd " we have an allusion to a character of this kind :

" I was," says the gay lampooner, " 'tother day at Will's, throwing out something of that nature ; and i' gad the hint

---

[1] In "An Exclamation against Julian, Secretary to the Muses; with the character of a libeller " he is addressed as the " common shore of this Poetick Town," and is said to gather his " well-pick'd Guineys " from a Dunghill. Further he is told : "All mischief's thine." In 1690 Julian went off to France.

was taken and out came that picture ; indeed the poor fellow was so civil as to present me with a dozen for my friends. I think I have one here in my pocket, would you please to accept it ? "

Julian's notoriety caused it to be said that at his death " lampoon felt a sensible decay ;" yet successors were numerous, and he had not at any time been without fellow-workers on the same lines. In the scurrilous pamphlet of 1673, we have a description of the town wit in the coffee house, and the " symptoms " of his disease are somewhat similar. To make a mockery of that which others hold sacred, and to shoot libels with forked tongue, are favourite employments of this poor misguided creature, who, in himself, falls so far short of reasoning power that " to discourse him seriously is to talk ethicks to a monkey." The writer's own display of coarseness helps to illustrate the charge brought against the coffee house as an institution, viz., that of raising into prominence certain pests of society whose natural insignificance might long have kept them harmless. The company at Will's has attracted the pen of the novelist, and Scott in his " Pirate " pictures yet humbler friends of the " Glorious John," whose highest honour was to be in his presence and to enjoy the privilege of applauding.

"They all laughed, and none louder than those who stood too far off to hear the jest; for everyone knew when he smiled there was something worth laughing at, and so took it upon trust."

Amongst them was Thimblethwaite the tailor, whose own wit was shown by his never quarrelling

"with any jest which wags who frequented that house were flinging about like squibs and crackers in a rejoicing night; and then, tho' some of the wits—ay, and I daresay the greater number, might have had some dealings with him in the way of trade, he never was the person to put any man of genius in unpleasant remembrance of such trifles."

Swift's satirical description of Will's and its learned coterie must find a place here, though it is by no means equally good-natured:

"The worst conversation I ever remember to have heard in my life was that at Will's coffee house, where the wits (as they were called) used formerly to assemble; that is to say, five or six men who had writ plays, or at least prologues, or had share in a miscellany, came thither, and entertained one another with their trifling composures, in so important an air as if they had been the noblest efforts of human nature, or that the fate of kingdoms depended on them; and they were usually attended with an humble audience of young students from the inns of court, or the universities; who, at due distance, listened to these oracles, and returned home with great contempt for their law and philosophy, their heads filled with trash, under the name of politeness, criticism, and belles-lettres." (Essay on Conversation.)

On the other hand, Steele has a more respectful mention of Will's in his first number of the *Tatler*, for he laments the alteration that had taken place there

"since Mr. Dryden frequented it; where you used to see songs, epigrams, and satires, in the hands of every man you met, you have now only a pack of cards ; and instead of the cavils about the turn of the expression, the elegance of the style, and the like, the learned now dispute only about the truth of the game."

However, in number 84 of the same paper, we have a quaint reference to one of the lesser wits,

"who a little after the Restoration writ an epigram with some applause, which he has lived upon ever since; and by virtue of it, has been a constant frequenter of this coffee house for forty years."

This old-established critic was somewhat jealous of Isaac Bickerstaff's fresher reputation.[1]

---

[1] The references to criticisms issuing from Will's are numerous. In 1693 a writer, the ill-success of whose play was attributed to Dryden's influence over the inferior critics at Will's, put it thus :

> From spawn of Will's, these wits of Future tense,
> He now appeals to men of riper sense.

And in "Urania's Temple" we have a reference to the former sign of Will's, the Cow. It is not, however, worth much as a description :

> A House there stands where once a Covent stood,
> A nursery still to the old Covent Brood.
>
> .   .   .   .   .   .
>
> Sometimes for Oracle yet more profound
> A titillating sonnets handed round, etc., etc., etc."

The reader will find references to these pamphlets in

Several of those who became well-known as poets or prose writers during the brilliant epoch of Queen Anne's reign, were proud of their early acquaintance with Dryden. Pope, whose education in every way fitted him to pay respect to the poet's principles and genius, represents himself as being brought to the coffee house for the privilege of listening to or even catching a sight of Dryden. To this occurrence, which probably took place in 1701 (this being the last year of Dryden's life, when Pope was not yet twelve years old), Johnson thus alludes :

"Who does not wish that Dryden could have known the value of the homage that was paid him, and foreseen the greatness of his young admirer ?"[1]

Scott's "Life of Dryden." The fate of William Urwin, or Irwin, the host at Will's, was decidedly unhappy, and is commemorated in a letter by Dennis, on the master having absconded for debt, dated from Will's, Nov. 5, 1695 :

> "Have you not heard
> These sounds upon the Cornish shore,—
> The sage Will Urwin is no more."

The above is here quoted from Malone, who mentions other lines (of 1691) addressed to "sage Will :"

> . . . thou that the town around
> For wit, and tea and coffee, art renown'd.

[1] Pope, who would probably be introduced by Henry Cromwell ("Honest, hatless, Cromwell"), an elderly fre-

Swift declares that the archcritic regretted to him the success of his own instructions, and found his readers made suddenly too skilful to be easily satisfied : a statement which may be coloured by resentment, for the younger author could not forget the stinging words, " Cousin Swift, you will never be a poet." However this may be, Dryden deliberately aimed at educating the public taste by means of the critical prefaces prefixed to his published plays. To some extent these prefaces were actually the result of conversations held at Will's, and in them the poet condescended to answer objections expressed in his presence at that coffee house. According to his latest biographer (Mr. Saintsbury in " English Men of Letters ") Dryden is to be regarded as a typical Englishman of his time ; also his works " contain the germs and

quenter of Will's, after all speaks somewhat disparagingly of Dryden as " a plump man with a down look, and not very conversible." He alludes to the incident in his first letter to Wycherley, which, says Mr. Leslie Stephen, is of doubtful authenticity. Malone, in his " Life of Dryden " (vol. i. pt. 1, p. 477, etc.), tells an anecdote of (Lord Chief Justice) Morley, who at an early period frequented Will's. The hero worshipper was outdone in enthusiasm by the poet himself. The latter, in return for a compliment upon his " Alexander's Feast," replied, " You are right, young gentleman, a nobler Ode never *was* produced, nor ever *will*."

indicate the direction of almost the whole literary movement for a century more." To this we may add, by way of corollary, that as Dryden's prose style gave later writers a clue to the art of easy composition, so his habitual presence at Will's was unconsciously imitated by the 18th century authors, who found in the leading coffee houses at once their topics, their inspiration and their reading public.

As already stated, the institution was fully developed in its essential features at the close of the 17th century, and the history of the later coffee houses does not form a part of our subject. The brilliant pages of both *Tatler* and *Spectator* abound with descriptions of particular coffee houses then most in fashion ; we know likewise that their social reputation was slow to become dimmed ; yet it is equally certain that some of the most interesting characteristics which had marked the earlier period were rapidly disappearing.

It remains to add a few words concerning what may be termed the free or voluntary system of coffee houses, and the peculiar social conditions which made it possible for these places to flourish for a while as open assemblies.

In some of the earliest specimens the company

was so ill-assorted as to afford much merriment to
onlookers, and even though the proceedings of
the Rota Club were sufficiently formal, yet it is
not likely that the Puritans would by themselves
have developed, out of that somewhat mechanical
arrangement, a really workable social institution.

It must also be noticed that the coffee house
was not as a rule frequented by persons of highest
rank; the "great courtier men," whose sayings
were retailed by gossip and minutely recorded
in memoirs of the Stuart period, seldom condescended to appear here in person. Yet the Restoration brought to London a number of adventurers,
whose purses did not enable them to support their
former pretensions to grandeur, and for these the
coffee house life, with its mixture of economy and
display, had an irresistible attraction. Amongst
such were to be found broken cavaliers of family,
who, still possessing a certain amount of influence,
were continually striving to regain a firm foothold
in society.[1]

---

[1] Such was the nature of the Assembly at Man's (see p.
156). After the Revolution, persons of highest distinction
no longer incurred suspicion by frequenting a coffee house.
Here too, on occasion, important state business might be
transacted (see the Journal of the Very Rev. R. Davies,
published by the Camden Society, under date of October

Others came here, as to a school of fashion, in order to pick up at second-hand the manners of a courtier; or, when French tastes and Dutch wars had rendered military costumes popular, to imitate the soldier's accent and gait, without undergoing the fatigues of a campaign. Self-respect does not seem to have prevented the middle classes from copying closely the dress and manners of their social superiors; accordingly. we find that a gold-laced coat and a carefully-selected wig carried a man far along the road to distinction, and enabled him to mix freely with very good company. To this preliminary test of fine clothing was presently added a mental qualification not quite so easily obtained. If the beau could write a copy of verses or manage to produce them with help from the scribblers at Will's, or even had the honour of a conversation with Mr. Dryden, and enjoyed the accompanying privilege of a pinch from his snuff-box, he was henceforth entitled to consider himself a "wit." In other words, a sort of literary test was coming into vogue, and

28th, 1689). Dean Davies was a regular frequenter of coffee houses; he might be found a second time on the same day at his favourite haunts, viz., Story's, St. Dunstan's and Shuttleworth's. The Illustration is taken from an edition of "Coffee House Jests" published in 1688.

a qualification of this kind, failing a more powerful introduction from some person of fashion, was
soon indispensable, if a man was not to be regarded
as an intruder in "the Wits" coffee house. As
regards political divisions, we have seen that these
were not of such a kind as to prevent free discussion in the generality of these places, where every
variety of opinion was tolerated, and when it was
only needful to have made up your mind so far as
to take one or other side in the friendly debate.
There were indeed other gaps seemingly impossible
to be bridged over, and at the same time rendering
unnecessary all artificial barriers : a stern Puritan
could not have been tempted to cast in his lot with
the fashionable nonentities at Man's, and the latter
would be equally careful to avoid places where
their style of conversation must have met with an
open rebuke. We have also seen that there were
coffee houses containing, at different times of the
day, guests who did not care to mingle, because
they had little or nothing in common. Whilst
Will's was able to boast of its literary associations, a stranger entering "the Grecian," so
famed for its connection with the "virtuosoes"
from Gresham and the Royal Society, would
feel it desirable to possess some previous acquain-

tance with these worthies or with their particular studies.

Within the coffee house, guests were not always upon an equality. Will's, like many of the early establishments, was up one flight of stairs. Here there was a regular gradation ; its balcony, or a seat near the fire-place during winter months, being the coveted place of honour. Two rooms were perhaps thrown into one to accommodate its numerous frequenters.[1]

Tables were set apart for divers topics. There is an odd reference to this in the Prologue to a Comedy of 1681 (quoted by Malone) :

> " In a coffee house just now among the rabble
> I bluntly asked, Which is the treason-table ?"

At Will's we read (Malone, vol. i. pt. 1, p. 477, etc.) of three divisions, viz., the Grave Club, the Witty Club, and the Rabble (Politicians) : of these last named the President was one Captain Swan. The President's chair, by the way, seems to have been quite an institution. In the case of the Rota,

---

[1] And this was probably the arrangement at Man's ; whereas in the distinctively business coffee houses separate rooms were provided at a later time for mercantile trans-actions. The introduction of wooden partitions—wooden boxes, as at a tavern—was also of somewhat later date.

we have seen that it was occupied by members in succession. A letter from Congreve to Walter Moyle in 1695 (as quoted by Malone) says :

" You wish yourself with us at Will's coffee house, and all here wish for you, from the President of the Grave Club to the most puny member of the Rabble."

Whilst, however, the principle of " each man to his taste " made the distinction between the different resorts very real, we are not to suppose that their usefulness as instruments of education for the average Londoner was spoiled by an over exactness in the matter of admission.

John Houghton, to whom we are indebted for the record of a quaint comparison between coffee houses and the university, after dealing fully with the business aspect of the question, adds that these places make all kinds of people sociable ; here the rich and the poor meet together, likewise the learned and the unlearned, whilst anyone in search of " good learning " or practical information has but to find out the right kind of coffee houses, viz., those frequented by the masters of that particular branch of knowledge which he affects, and " he may in short space gain the pith and marrow of the others' reading and studies." [1]

[1] Even in his day candour compelled Houghton to admit

We may conclude this story of the origin and growth of coffee houses by giving some account of a desperate attempt to extend their influence by combining their functions with those of journalism. In order to do so, we must step beyond the limit of our period. It will not be uninteresting to the reader to see to what extent evils already latent have developed within the short space of thirty years.

The nature of this enterprise is discussed in a piece of criticism entitled " The Case between the Proprietors of Newspapers and the Coffee Men of London and Westminster, fairly stated ": " For a People to sound their own Praise, as being more wise and sagacious than the rest of the world, may justly be called a Vanity . . . yet our coffee men are so vain as to think they can furnish the Town with something more extraordinary than what they are at present Masters of." This

that too many made an ill use of these places, and, as time went on, the whole system was effectively undermined. The attempt of which we are about to give an account was unfortunate in being made just when the mania for gin, a comparatively new importation, was nearly at its height. The coffee house keepers were either obliged to suffer in pocket from this fresh attraction, or participate in the sale of it and bring themselves into disrepute.

reference to the wise man's warning about the inconvenience of searching out one's own glory, was provoked by the self-laudatory tone of a former pamphlet, called, " The case of the Coffee Men against the Newswriters." In this quaint document (dated 1729,—the originals of both are in the British Museum) it was stated as an intolerable grievance that newspapers were choked with advertisements, and filled with foolish stories picked up at all places of public entertainment, including the ale-houses; and "persons are employed—one or two for each paper—at so much a week to haunt coffee houses, and thrust themselves into companies where they are not known . . . . in order to pick up matter for the papers." The remedy, as we shall presently see, promised a vast increase of custom and popularity to the coffee house keepers, and would lead to a kind of monopoly in journalism.

This bitter complaint is met by the critic with still more serious charges concerning the " flagrant scandalous and growing impositions of the coffee houses upon the public "; a hint is dropped concerning the questionable characters of the young women employed at the bar; "the impudence of the coffee boys is likewise insupportable," and altogether the state of these places is such as to " bring the best of gentlemen into contempt."

The genuineness of the coffee men's appeal on behalf of truth is treated with a great amount of scorn. Since men of business and men of pleasure—" of which the company resorting to the coffee houses is entirely compounded—never mind or remember anything that is above a day's standing," it is absurd to provide them with that which requires any patience to examine. No credit is to be given to

" the formal story of the Public's being impos'd upon with Lyes and Fictions, instead of News. Suppose this were true, what is that to the Coffee Men? Were it not for the Follies, Vices, and Extravagancies contain'd in the Papers, how would the company who resort to their houses employ themselves?"

The news vendors add to the charge of short-sightedness an amusing indictment on the score of ingratitude, and present us with a lively picture of the dangers to which " members of the Press " were exposed in the pursuit of their honourable calling :

" The collectors of News, 'tis true, gather up most of their Intelligence from Coffee houses ; but what of that? They pay for their coffee, and very often run the Hazard of broken

Bones into the Bargain ; which I think a sufficient argument to entitle them to the Property of the Papers."

When one considers the audacity of the coffee men's plea, there is little room to wonder at the shout of derision which followed. It amounted in effect to the following proposal : The country has now for many years enjoyed the advantages and bemoaned the excesses occasioned by the Freedom of the Press. The public have learnt to believe in the singleness of purpose displayed by the chief supporters of its liberty, viz., the coffee men of London : now is the opportunity of rewarding their eminent services in the past, and of securing their future aid against those pests of society—the unlicensed news vendors. What the Government has attempted in the way of restriction, and has signally failed to accomplish, might yet be effected by means of a joint understanding between the English nation and the Coffee House Masters. In the words of the patent once granted to Roger L'Estrange, 'the sole right of intelligence' must be forthwith handed over to those who alone are certain not to abuse the public confidence.

Nor is the scheme set forth in mere outline, but forms a practical design complete down to the veriest details. The editors of the *Tatler* and

Spectator had indeed made the coffee house the scene of some of their most brilliant pages, and the former fancifully dated his papers from such of these places as were famed for particular subjects ; but here we have a new departure, and the proposed coffee house Gazette is to be regularly supplied with authentic information obtained upon the spot. For this purpose each establishment will be provided, as some of them already were, with a brass slate or ivory tablet having a pencil attached thereto. These slates are to be filled by gentlemen frequenters of the house with such articles of news as each may be able to afford, and, in order to secure to the public promptness as well as trustworthy intelligence, the slates will be called for twice in the day by persons duly authorized and connected with the journal.

Such, then, is the somewhat primitive proposal by which the public are to write their own newspapers ; the customers are to be flattered by seeing their compositions in print on the following day; the coffee house keeper will henceforth place in his pocket the profits of the paper as well as the ordinary takings of his house. It would seem that, for whatever reason, the plan was not put into action, and nothing ever came of a great gathering of coffee house keepers, which was to meet and deliberate upon the steps to be taken.

Yet we must allow these men credit for perceiving one defect in the coffee house system— a defect so closely connected with its highest achievement as not to admit of a remedy. This much may be gathered from the admission that the places in question are liable to the intrusion of impertinent fellows, who thrust themselves into companies where they are not known, and where they certainly are not wanted.

A strict degree of privacy was not at any time possible in a resort of this kind, and the growing desire to exclude unwelcome visitors doubtless led to many a " coffee house scuffle." As an appeal to brute force was certainly not in keeping with the progress of society, so it did not always succeed; a bevy of lacqueys might prove insufficient to bar the entrance to Man's, and this protection was not often at hand in the case of lesser establishments. When once the voluntary system had broken down, a fresh device was necessary, in order that society might be protected from such incursions, and against the still more dangerous presence of adventurers, whose desperate character and ruffianly intentions were masked by a fashionable exterior. Constant frequenters of houses of entertainment, where the custom had prevailed of laying down a small sum upon entrance, now united, and by means of a regular payment were able to secure the whole or a part of the premises to themselves ; in this simple manner was developed an institution better suited to the exclusive tendencies of the average Londoner, and we may date the widespread popularity of subscription clubs from the period when coffee houses began to decline. The day was passing in which, for a short while, publicity had been prized as, to use the words of Aubrey, "the modern advantage of coffee houses in this great city, before which men knew not how to be acquainted but with their own relations and societies."

In a partial revival of our own time, not many of the distinctive features of the coffee house may be recognized ; attempts are sometimes made in places bearing this name to imitate the social conditions of tavern life, whilst in others a return is made to the primitive simplicity of the days when coffee first became known in this country. They have one and all ceased to be centres of literary activity. Some of the old traditions are likely enough to be revived, yet we cannot venture to say whether the coffee house will again in any degree occupy its peculiar social position, midway between the open tavern and the private club. To be reasonably select, and yet so far inclusive as to bring together all those who have something in common, and to induce them to lay aside for a while the reserve habitual to our nation— this would be its ideal. The success of the coffee house in realizing such an ideal must always appear remarkable to later and less fortunate Englishmen.

BIBLIOGRAPHY.

Wa. Rumsey. Organon Salutis, an instrument to cleanse the stomach, as also divers new experiments on Tobacco and Coffee, 1657. *The 2nd ed., 1659, was printed for D. Pakeman at the Rainbow, and contains letters from Sir H. Blunt and James Howel.*

Dr. Edw. Pococke, *translator.* The Nature of the drink Kauhi or Coffee, and the berry of which it is made. Described by an Arabian Physician. *A single sheet with the Arabic facing, Oxford,* 1659.

The Censure of the Rota, upon Mr. Milton's book, entituled, the ready and easie way to establish a Free Commonwealth, 1660. *For Rota pamphlets, see pp.* 81, 100, 101.[1]

A Character of Coffee and Coffee-houses, by W. P. [*See Hazlitt's Handbook to Pop. Lit.*], 1661.

The Coffee Scuffle; occasioned by a contest between a learned knight and a pitifull Pedagogue, with the character of a coffee-house. Printed and are to be sold at the Salmon Coffee House, neer the Stocks Market, 1662. *Verses by* [?] *Woolnoth on Sir J. Langham and Evans, a schoolmaster.*

The Vertues of Coffee. Set forth in the works of the Lord Bacon, his Natural Hist., Mr. Parkinson his Herbel. . . . 1663.

---

[1] In Grey's edition of *Hudibras,* 1801, *p.* 98, the ' Rota' is mentioned as one of a *Collection of Loyal Songs, vol. ii., pp.* 214, 215. The ballads of 1684–5 have references to *zealots* who *are coffee new plots divine,* but do not include the Rota song.

The Coffee Mans Granado discharged upon the Maidens Complaint against COFFEE. In a Dialogue . . . *verse,* 1663.

A Cup of Coffee, or Coffee in its colours, *verse,* 1663.

The Character of a Coffee House . . . by an Eye and Ear Witness, 1665.

P. [F.]. De potu coffi. *Francof.* 1666.

Tarugo's wiles [*or, The Coffee House*] as it was acted at his Highness's, the Duke of York's Theatre, 1667.

News from the Coffee House, in which is shewn their several sorts of passions . . . 1667. *Reprinted in* 1672, *as The Coffee House or Newsmongers' Hall.*

Robert Morton. *Lines appended to* The Nature, Quality and most Excellent Vertues of Coffee. ? 1670. *For similar bills of* 1660 *etc., see pp.* 65, 85.

P. S. Du Four, *translator.* De l'usage du Caphé, *from the Latin* [?] *of H. L. Strauss, c.* 1660, *Lyon,* 1671.

Magri Domenico. Virtù del Kafé . . . seconda impressione con aggiunta. *Rom.* 1671.

F. Nairo Banesius. De Saluberrima Potione Cahve seu Cafe . . . *Rom.* 1671.

A Broadside against Coffee; or the Marriage of the Turk, *verse,* 1672.

The Character of a Coffee House, with the Symptoms of a Town-Wit, 1673.

A brief description of the excellent Vertues of that sober and wholesome drink called COFFEE, 1674.

The Women's Petition against Coffee, representing to public Consideration the grand inconvenienc(i)es accruing to their sex from the excessive use of the drying and enfeebling Liquor, 1674.

The Mens Answer to the Womens Petition against Coffee vindicating . . . their Liquor, from the undeserved aspersion lately cast upon them, in their Scandalous Pamphlet, 1674.

Coffee Houses Vindicated in answer to the late published Character . . . with the Grand Conveniency of such Civil places of resort and ingenious Conversation, 1675.

The Ale Wives Complaint against the Coffee-houses, in a Dialogue between a Victualler's wife and a coffee man, being at difference about spiriting each others trade. [*See Hazlitt*], 1675.

By the King. A Proclamation for the Suppression of Coffee Houses, 1675.

By the King. An Additional Proclamation concerning Coffee Houses, 167$\frac{5}{6}$.

Coffee House Jests. *Contains scarcely anything relating to Coffee Houses*, 1677.

A Coffee House Dialogue, 1679. *A Continuation was also published.*

Henry Mundy, M.D., Oxon., βιοχρησтολογία. *See Cap. xiv. De Coffâ*, 1680.

The Natural History of Coffee. . . . *Quotations from Tavernier, etc.*, 1682.

P. S. Du Four. *See under* 1671. Traitez Nouveaux et Curieux du Café. . . . *Lugd.* 1683, [*so Douglas; see ed.* 1685, *same year translated into Latin by S. Spon*], also *La Haye*, 3e ed., 1693.

John Chamberlain, F.R.S., *translator.* The manner of making of coffee, tea . . . *special heading*, Of the Use of Coffee; *See Du Four*, 1671, 1685.

Rebellious Antidote : or a Dialogue between Coffee and Tea, *verse*, 1685.

Nic. de Blegny. Le Bon Usage du Thé du Caffé et du Chocolat . . . *Paris*, 1687.

Cornelius Bontekoe. Tractaat Van het Excellenste Kruyd The Coffi en Chocolate. *Amster.* 1689. [*See Douglas.*]

The School of Politicks, Or the Humours of a Coffee House. A Poem. 1690. *cf. a Play, with the latter title, by Ned Ward, published,* 1707.

Angelo Rambaldi. Ambrosia Arabica . . . Cafe discorso, *Bologna,* 1691.

Sir T. Pope Blount. A Natural History . . . *See pp.* 107, *etc., etc.,* 1693.

Sir Hans Sloane. Account of the Coffee Shrub. *Phil. Trans. Vol. xvii., p.* 603, 1694. *See vol. xxi. p.* 311, *for Houghton's account* [*For Houghton, Bradley, etc., see Appen. B*], *also* 1684, *p.* 44, *for account by Sir Thomas Smith.*

J. B. Rousseau. Caffé, *le Comédie, Paris,* 1694. [*See Barbier, Ouvrages Anon.*].

Antoine Galland. De l'Origine et du Progrez du Café. Sur un Manuscrit Arabe de la Bibliotheque du Roy. *Caen,* 1699. *See also Chrestomathie arabe, ed. by Silvestre de Sacy.*

APPENDIX.

A. *See page* 83 *note.*

The following regulation occurs amongst the Statuta Academica, of which a copy, suspended by a chain, is to this day carried in front of the proctors at certain University functions:

Nov. 9, 1664. It is ordered that all in pupillari statu that shall go to coffee-houses without their *tutors* leave shall be punished according to the statute for haunters of taverns and alehouses. *Stat. Acad. Cantab. p.* 494, *Decreta Præfectorum.* I am indebted to J. Bass Mullinger, Esq., of St. John's College, Cambridge, for drawing my attention to the above, and for the following quotation from the series of questions sent in 1675 by the Duke of Monmouth, the Chancellor, to the Vice-Chancellor and Heads of Colleges :

12. Whether the coffee-houses be much frequented or not, by what sort and degree of men, and at what hour ?

Ans. The coffee-houses are daily frequented and in great numbers of all sorts (the heads of houses and other doctors excepted) at all hours, especially morning and evening.

Stat. Acad. Cantab. pp. 302–4.

B. *See page* 90, *note.*

A Broad-Side against Coffee; or the Marriage of the Turk.

Coffee a kind of Turkish Renegade,
Has late a match with Christian water made ;
At first between them happened a Demur,
Yet joined they were but not without great *stir;*

.   .   .   .   ,   .   .

Coffee was cold as Earth, water as Thames ;
And stood in need of recommending Flames ;
Coffee so brown as berry does appear,
Too swarthy for a Nymph so fair, so clear :
And yet his sails he did for England hoist,
Though cold and dry, to court the cold and moist ;

.   .   .   .

A Coachman was the first (here) Coffee made,
And ever since the rest drive on the trade ;
Me no good Engalash ! and sure enough,
He plaid the Quack to salve his Stygian stuff ;
Ver boon for de Stomach, de Cough, Ptifick,
And I believe him, for it looks like Physick.
Coffee a crust is charkt into a coal,
The smell and taste of the Mock China bowl ;

.   .   .   .

And yet they tell you that it will not burn,
Though on the jury blisters you return ;
Whose furious heat does make the water rise,
And still thro' the alembics of your eyes.
Dread and desire you fall to't snap by snap,
As starving dogs do scalding porridge lap.
But to cure drunkards it has got great fame ;

.   .   .   .

And now alas ! the Drench has credit got,
And he's no Gentleman that drinks it not ;
That such a Dwarf should rise to such a stature !
But custom is but a remove from Nature.
A little Dish and a large Coffee House,
What is it but a Mountain and a Mouse ?

> Mens humana novitatis avidissima,
> London, printed for I.M. Anno Dom. 1672.

Authorities from whom the account in the text, *pp.* 86–91
is derived :

(1) John Houghton, F.R.S., whose 'Collection for the Improvement of Husbandry and Trade,' *see ed. of* 1727, was revised by Bradley. Writing on May 2nd, 1701, he says, 'Bowman's apprentices were first John Painter [*see Appendix F*], then Humphry, from whose wife I had this account.' Likewise Houghton says that 'one Rastall, whom I knew, and within these few days I saw' was [*in* 1651] at the Coffee-house in Leghorn, whither came Pasqua and Mr. Edwards; moreover, 'Mr. Rastall found them [*i.e. Pasqua and Bowman*]' together 'in 1654.' [*In Houghton's 'Collection,' ed. of* 1692, *No.* 23, *is a notice that 'Coffee-men and others' who buy the paper in large quantities, do so 'with liberty to return those that won't sell.'*] See also Phil. Trans. Vol. xxi., p. 311.

(2) R. Bradley, Professor of Botany, at Cambridge. Writing in 1721, '*The Virtue and Use of Coffee, with regard to the Plague,*' he quotes 'a letter written at that time by a curious Gentleman, who lately communicated it to me.' In the 'Appendix to New Improvements' he speaks of 'my Treatise of Coffee published in the year 1714, when I was in Holland.' This was 'A short historical Account of Coffee,' and it is quoted by Douglas, *e.g. the verses on Pasqua, see pp.* 89, 90; I am not aware that the original book is still in existence.

(3) Dr. Douglas, F.R.S., quotes from Houghton and Bradley in his 'Arbor Yemensis fructum Cofè ferens : or, a Description and History of the Coffee Tree,' with 'a Supplement,' 1725, *as given by Watt., see ed.* 1727. He also received information concerning the earliest coffee-houses from Elford, junr., and from Constantine of the 'Grecian.'

(4) John Aubrey, see Appendix C.

C. *See page* 93, *note.*

The late Mr. T. C. Noble, in his *Memorials of Temple Bar,* says the Wardmote Inquest presentment of December 21st, "has been often quoted, but the entry in the records has never been given in its complete form.   It runs thus :—

'Disorders and Annoys. Item, we pr'sent James Ffarr, barber, for makinge and selling of a drink called coffee, whereby in makeing the same, he annoyeth his neighbrs. by evil smells and for keeping of ffier for the most pt. night and day, whereby his chimney and chambr. hath been sett on ffire, to the great danger and affrightment of his neighbrs. Witness and compts. Mr. Ro. Meade, Mr. John Rae, Mr. Daniel Pakeman, Mr. William Leake and Widd. Lashley.'

Mr. Noble mentions the three following booksellers as keeping their shops at the Rainbow : Ephm. Dawson, 1636 ; D. Pakeman, 1650; Sl. Speed, 1662. James Farr died in the year 1681.

Aubrey says of Sir Henry Blunt, ' He is now neer or altogether 80 yeares, his intellectualls good still, and body pretty strong.' The following passage from the ' Lives ' has, through the kindness of the Librarian, been compared with the original in the Bodleian. [*Aubrey MS.* 6, *fol.* 102.]

" Since he was . . . yeare old he dranke nothing but water or coffee. . . .

" When coffee first came in he was a great upholder of it, and hath ever since been a constant frequenter of coffee-houses, especially Mr. Farres, at the Rainbowe, by Inner Temple gate, and lately John's coffee house in Fuller's Rents. The first coffee house in London was in St. Michael's Alley in Cornehill, opposite to the church, which was sett up by one . . . Bowman, *coachman to Mr. Hodges a Turkey merchant, who putt him upon it,* in or about the yeare 1652. 'Twas about four yeares before any other was sett up ; and that was by Mr. Far.

" Jonathan Paynter [*opposite*] to St. Michs. church was the first apprentice to the Trade : viz. to Bowman. M[e]mdm the Bagneo in Newgate street was built and first opened in Decemb., 1679, built by . . . Turkish merchants." This was written by Aubrey about 1680 ; at the end he added : " This last weeke of Sept. 1682 he was taken very ill at London . . . and removed to Titting-hanger."

Burn quotes from *The Complaisant Companion*, 1674, *p*. 54, the following version of the St. Alban's hoax ; he has, however, confused Sir Henry, the true author of the jest, with Sir Thomas Pope Blount. *See Bibliography*, 1693.

" Two Jesuits seated in a coffee-house told a great many foreign stories, which [*Sir Henry Pope Blount*] a gentleman and a great traveller sitting by knew to be notorious lyes, yet contradicted them not, but told one of his own making, which was, that now is to be seen at St. Alban's a stone trough, which that Saint kept a long time for water for his ordinary use, and that ever since if swine should eat anything out of it they would die instantly." The Jesuits rode to St. Alban's and, on their return, taxed Sir Henry with an untruth ; to whom he replied, " ' Gentlemen, I thought you had been more civill ; you told me the other night a hundred palpable lyes, and I went not about to disprove you ; I told you but one, and you, by your own confession, have ridden twenty miles to do it.' "

D. *See page* 97.

In addition to his list of opponents, Aubrey says of the Rota-men, " the room was every evening full as it could be crammed. I cannot now recount the whole number ; . . . There was Mr. Hen. Nevill, Major Wildman, Mr. . . . Wooseley of . . . Staffordsh., Mr. Coke, gr.-son of Sir Edw., Sir William Poulteney, *chaire-man*, Mr. Maximilian Petty, *a very able man in these matters, and who had more than once turned the Councill-board of O. Cromwell, his kinsman*, M. . . Carteret, of Garneley, . . . Cradoc, a merchant, Mr. Hen. Ford, Major Venner, M. Edward Baghshaw, . . . Croon M.D. cum multis aliis, now slipt out of my memory, which were auditors as well as myself.

Wood, in his Life of Harrington, copies, almost word for word, this description of the Rota. He adds Aubrey's name to the list of those who attended, also Rob. Wood of Lincoln College, and ' Jam. Ardenne, a Divine.'

Pepys' list is as follows : " Jany. 10th. To the coffee house where were a great confluence of gentlemen : viz. Mr. Harrington, Poultney, chairman, Gold [*a well-known merchant*], Dr. Petty, &c., where admirable discourse till nine at night."

E. *See page* 119.

THE CHARACTER OF A COFFEE-HOUSE. . . . BY AN EYE AND EAR WITNESS.

> When Coffee once was vended here,
> The Alc'ron shortly did appear :
> Four *our Reformers were such Widgeons*
> New liquors brought in new Religions.

Printed in the year 1665.

> A Coffee House, the learned hold
> It is a place where Coffee's sold;
> This derivation cannot fail us,
> For where Ale's vended that's and Ale-house.

> .   .   .   .   .   .

> And if you see the great Morat
> With shash on's head instead of hat,
> Or any Sultan in his dress,
> Or picture of a Sultaness,
> Or John's admir'd curled pate
> Or th' Great Mogul in's Chair of State.
> Or Constantine the Grecian,
> Who fourteen years was th' only man
> That made Coffee for the great Bashaw
> Although the man he never saw :

Or if you see a Coffee-cup
Fil'd from a Turkish pot, hung up
Within the clouds, and round it pipes,
Wax candles, stoppers,—these are types
And certain signs *with many more*
Would be too long to write them 'ore
Which plainly do spectators tell
That in that house they Coffee sell.
Some wiser than the rest *no doubt*
Say they can by the smell find't out:
In at a door *say they* but thrust
Your nose, and if you scent burnt Crust,
Be sure there's coffee sold that's good,
For so by most 'tis understood.
Now being entered, there's no needing
Of compliments or gentile breeding,
For you may seat you any where,
There's no respect of persons there.

.   .   .   .   .   .

But if you ask, what good does Coffee.
He'l answer, Sir, don't think I scoff ye,
If I affirm there's no disease
Men have that drink it but find ease.

.   .   .   .   .   .

There stands another holds his head
Ore the Coffee-pot, was almost dead
Even now with Rhume; ask him he'll say
That all his Rhume's now past away.
See, there's a man sits now demure
And sober, was within this hour
Quite drunk, and comes here frequently,
For 'tis his daily malady.

.   .   .   .   .   .

As from the top of Paul's high steeple
Th' whole city's viewed, even so all people

May here be seen : no secrets are
At the Court for Peace, or th' Camp for war,
But straight they're here disclos'd and known.

   .   .   .   .

Here at a Table sits *perplext*
A griping Usurer and next
To him a gallant Furioso
Then nigh to him a Virtuoso ;
A Player then, *full fine* sits down,
And close to him a Country Clown.
O' th' other side sits some Pragmatick
And next to him some sly Phanatick.
The gallant he for Tea doth call,
The Usurer for nought at all.
Pragmatick he doth intreat
That they will fill him some Beau-Cheat
The Virtuoso he cries hand me
Some Coffee mixt with Sugar Candy.
Phanaticus at last says come
Bring me some Aromaticum.
The Player bawls for Chocolate,
All which the Bumpkin wondering at.
Cries, ho, my Masters, what d'ye speak,
D'ye call for drink in Heathen Greek :
Give me some good old Ale or Beer,
Or else I will not drink, I swear

   .   .   .   .   .

The Curioso
      . . . thus begins, Sirs, unto me
It reason seems that liberty
Of speech and words should be allowed
Where men of differing judgments crowd,
And that's a Coffee House, for where
Should men discourse so free as there ?

Coffee and Commonwealth begin
Both with one letter, both came in
Together for a Reformation
To make's a free and sober nation.
Here in a corner sits a Phantick
And there stands by a frisking Antick—
Of all sorts some and all conditions,
Even Vintners, Surgeons, and Physicians.
The blind, the deaf, and aged cripple
Do here resort and Coffee tipple.

.	.	.	.	.	.

Truth is, old poets beat their brains
To find out high and lofty strains
To praise the *now too frequent* use
Of the bewitching grapes strong juice.

.	.	.	.	.	.

Only poor Coffee seems to me
No subject fit for poetry.
At least 'tis one that none of mine is
So I do wave't and here write—

FINIS.

F.	*See pp.* 141, 142, *note.*

In the Record Office, amongst the State Papers, *Domestic Series—reference in Calendar, vol. xlvii.* 118, is the following list of seven persons to be found at certain Coffee-houses :—

'John Ravermet, at the Coffee House in Bedford Street, Covent Garden. Jim Child, at the west end of Pauls. John Painter,[1] in Cornhill. John Davies, next door to Mr.

---

[1] John or Jonathan [*see Appendix C*] Painter, Bowman's first apprentice, was out of his time in 1664, and was afterwards in partnership with Bowman's other apprentice in St. Peter's Alley, Cornhill. Possibly the stock-jobbers' famous

Blagiards to Crown Tavern over against the old [*i.e. Royal*] Exchange. Captain Chillington, at Leaden Hall Coffee House. Maddison, Wills Coffee House, in St. Michaels Alley. Mr. Merman, at the Coffee House in St. Martin le Grand.'

The list is endorsed " Mr. Muddiman s office

Coffee house[*s*]

N.B.—The manuscript is torn, so that the above letter s is only conjectural on my part. On the back of the paper is written in pencil "found un[*der*] 1661."

---

coffee house, in Exchange Alley, took its name from him. Jonathan's is mentioned in the Journal of Dean Davies, Ap. 9, 1690. It occurs, at an earlier period, on Dangerfield's list, *see p.* 173.

COFFEE HOUSE TOKENS.[1]

APPENDIX G. *See pp.* 144–148.

ABCHURCH LANE.

Avgvstine . Rand.—Hand pouring coffee into a cup.
Rev. In . Abchvrch Lane.—His
half peny.

ALDERSGATE STREET.

* *Solyman*—Sultan's head.
Rev. The . Coffee . House . in .
Aldersgate . Street . 1666.

Edw. Ward, in his *London Spy*,
1709 (*commenced in* 1698), *pt. xii.*,
p. 275, *etc.*, mentions that this 'Ancient fabrick, by antiquity made
venerable,' was frequented by doctors with a turn for politics, and
by Puritans who wished to recall
the days of Cromwell. Here, too,
a certain talker was wont to 'illustrate the story, *Sir Harry Blunt
like*, with some few advantages.'

The above token was probably
issued by R. Ward. See under
Bread Street.

Solyman II., son of Selim I.,
began to reign in 1520. He was
one of the most fierce and renowned
of Turkish conquerors. He died,
at the age of 76, in 1566.

BARBICAN.

* Robert . Hayes . at . yᵉ . Coffe .
Hovs.—Turk's head.
*Rev. In . Barbican . formerly .
in . Pannyer . Ally.*

For reference to a murder committed here in 1672, *vide* Smyth's
"Obituary" (Camden Society, 44),
p. 95.

**BARTHOLOMEW CLOSE, SMITH-
FIELD.**

Richard . Kempe, 1666.—Turk's
head between R. K.
Rev. In S . Bartholomew . Close.
—His halfe penny.

* William . Rvssell . 1671.—His
Coffee Hovse.
Rev. In . S[t] . Bartholmews .
Close. — Coffee-man pouring
coffee.

BASINGHALL STREET.

*Richard . Buckland . in . Basing-
hall . Street.*
Rev. Turk seated smoking : a
man standing, presenting him
a cup.

---

[1] For a list of these, and of all other tokens belonging to the same
period, readers are referred to Mr. G. C. Williamson's revised edition
of Boyne (London section, edited by Mr. G. E. Hodgkin). See also
catalogues by J. H. Burn and J. Y. Akerman.

* An asterisk denotes that the description has been verified, with the
help of Mr. E. M. Borrajo, from the original token in the Beaufoy Cabinet,
Guildhall. I would likewise acknowledge the co-operation of Mr.
Warwick Wroth, Assistant in the Department of Coins and Medals,
British Museum.

BELL YARD, FLEET STREET.
Iacob . Lions . in . Bell . Yard.
—Turk's head between I. L.
Neare . Temple . Barr . 1666.—
His half peny.

BETHLEM (BISHOPSGATE WITH-
OUT).
Iohn . Clapton . at . the.— Hand
pouring coffee into a pot.
Rev. Coffee . Hovse . in . Bethe-
lem.—His penny, 1669.

BISHOPSGATE STREET.
Hen . Wellington . near . yᵉ .
Post.—Hand pouring coffee.
Rev. Hovs . in . Bishopsgate .
Street.—CoffeeHovse,W.H.W.
See under *Checquer Yard.*

BREAD STREET.
Solyman.—Turk's head.
*Rev. Wards . Coffee . Hovse . in .
Bread . Street,* 1671.
The specimen in the British Mu-
seum is of the large brass size.

BROAD STREET.
*Siluester . Deane . His . Halfe .
Penny.*
Rev. In . Brod . Street . 1667.—
Hand pouring coffee.

BULL AND MOUTH STREET.
Drings . Coffee . Hovse . in . —
Hand pouring coffee.
Rev. Bvll . and . Movth . Street .
by.—Alldersgate . 1671.

CANNON STREET.
* Anne . Blvnt . in . — Turk's
head.
Rev. Cannon . Street . 1672.—
1ᵈ amid eight rosettes.

In this year ' divers persons who
presumed . . . to stamp, coin,
exchange, and distribute, farthings, half-pence, and pence of
brass and copper' were ' taken into
custody, in order to a severe prosecution ;' but, upon submission, their
offences were forgiven, and it was

not until the year 1675 that the
private tokens finally ceased to be
current. See *Burn's Introduction.*
p. xxxiii., &c.

This is not the only instance of a
woman's name standing by itself on
a Coffee House Token. The *City
Quaeries for* 1660 makes mention
of a ' She-Coffee-Merchant.'

CARTER LANE.
Tho . Ovtridge . at . Carter.—
Hand holding cup over table
on which are a cup and two
pipes.
Rev. Lane . end . near . Creed .
Lane.—Turk's head, 1ᵈ.
This token, like many others of
the period, is of an octangular shape.
The couple of short pipes are of the
same character as those so often
dug up in our London excavations.
[Akerman.]

In describing a token issued at
Leeds, Boyne (Yorkshire Tokens,
p. 13) says, ' The pipes on this and
other Tokens are of the kind called
by the vulgar " Fairy Pipes." . . .
When perfect [they] are about eight
inches long, thicker in the stem
than modern pipes, with small heads
almost egg-shaped.' See under
Spitalfields.

CATEATON STREET.
George . Francklin.— Bust of a
Turk holding a cup. *
Rev. In . Cateaten . Streete.—
His half peny.

CHANCERY LANE.
* *George Dayhin.*—Turk's head.
*Rev. Att . the . Coffee . House .
in . Chancery . Lane.*

*Joh . Rider . at . ye . Coffee .
House . at . the . Rolls . Gate .
in . Chancery . Lane.*
Rev. His . half . peny. — Turk's
head.

* *Robert Terrey* . *His* . ½d. —
Turk's head.
Rev. Att . *the* . *Coffee* . *House* .
Chancery . *Lane.*

From *The Newes, No.* 73, *Sept.*
7*th,* 1665, it appears that "an excellent Electuary and Drink" was
sold by "Robert Terry, at the
coffee house in Chancery Lane."
[Williamson.]

CHEAPSIDE.
* Charles . Kiftell.—Hand pouring coffee.
Rev. At . the . Coffee . Hovse .
in . Cheap . Side . 1669.

CHECQUER YARD.
H. Wellington . at . yᵉ . Coffe .
Hovs.—Hand pouring coffee.
H.W.
Rev. In . Checquer . Yard . by .
Dowgate. — His halfe penny,
1665.

CLARE MARKET.
Iohn . Renob . Coffee = 1ᵈ.
Rev. Hovse . in . Newmarket =
I.R.

CORNHILL.
Robert . Halton.—A man seated
holding cup, into which a servant pours coffee.
Rev. In . Cornhill = R.E.H.

* Vnion in Cornhil.—In small
compartment, the figure 3.
Rev. Blank.

Struck on leather. There is another specimen in the British Museum which has the figure 4.

DUNNING'S ALLEY, BISHOPSGATE
WITHOUT.
Iohn . Stanton . in . Dvnings.—
Hand pouring coffee.
Rev. Ally . withovt . Bishop-
gate.—His halfe penny, 1668.

ROYAL EXCHANGE.
At . the . Globe . Coffee . House.
—A globe on a stand.
Rev. On . the . back . side of .
the . Royall . Encheng.

'There is a Parcel of Coffee-Berry
to be put to publique sale upon
Wednesday, the 23 . instant, at 6
a clock in the evening at the Globe
Coffee-house at the end of St.
Bartholomew-Lane, over against
the North Gate of the Royall Exchange. . . And if any desire to be
further informed they may repair
to Mr. Brigg, Publique Notary at
the said Globe Coffee-house.'—
The Intelligencer, December 21,
1663. [Boyne.]

From *The Advertiser,* May 19—
26, 1657, we learn that in Bartholomew Lane, on the back side
of the Old Exchange, the drink
called coffee is to be sold in the
morning, and at three of the clock
in the afternoon. [E. F. King.]

To the south of the Exchange
competition was keen : 'At the
Exchange Ally from Cornhill into
Lumber Street neer the Conduit, at
the Musick-Room belonging to the
Palsgrave's Hall, is sold by retayle
the right coffee powder : likewise
that termed the Turkey Berry, well
cleansed at 30*d.* per pound. . . the
East India berry (so called) of the
best sorts at 20*d.* per pound, of
which at present in divers places
there is very bad, which the ignorant
for cheapness do buy, and is the
chief cause of the now bad coffee
drunk in many plaies [*sic*].'—*Kingdom's Intelligencer,* June 5, 1662.

N.B.—An advertisement issued
from the sign of the Great Turk
(house seal, *Morat*), is similar,
though the prices are slightly different.

*The . Coffee . House . in . Ex-
chang . Alley.*
Rev.   Morat.—A Sultan's head.

There are two specimens of this
token in the British Museum ; one,
being struck in silver, was probably
a proof from the die, and not intended for circulation.

Amurath IV., called Morat or
Morad, reigned from 1623 to 1640.
He took Bagdad after it had resisted
the efforts of the Turks for fifty
years; his glory was sullied by an
indiscriminate massacre of Persians.
He granted Muslims permission to
sell and drink wine publicly ; but
this edict caused scandal and was
withdrawn after two years.

Morat, an Indian despot, is a
conspicuous character in Dryden's
Aureng-zebe ; but the play was not
acted until 1676, when tokens had
ceased.   The two Morats have no
more connection than has Solyman
Aga (mentioned in the same play)
with the Turkish Emperor whom
Ward commemorates on his tokens.

* Morat ye Great men did mee
   call.—Face, to left.
Rev.   Where   eare   I   came   I
   conqver'd all.—*Coffee, Tobacco,
   Sherbet,   Tea,   &   Chocolat,
   Retal'd in Exchange Ally.*

* Morat . y^e . Great . men . did .
   mee . call.—Sultan's head.
Rev.   Where . eare . I . came .
   I . conqver'd . all.—*Coffee, To-
   bacco, Sherbet, Tea, Chocolat,
   Retail, in Exchange Alee.*

* Morat ye Great men did mee
   call.—Face, to left.
Rev.   Where eare I *came* I conqver'd *all.—Coffee, Chocolat,
   Tea, Sherbett, & Tobac sould
   in Exchaing Alley.*

The specimen in the British Museum looks as though it had been
cast in a mould.

FLEET STREET.
   * Iames . Farr . 1666.—An arched
   rainbow based on clouds.
   Rev.   In . Fleet . Street = His
   half peny.

FRIDAY STREET.
   * Andrew . Vincent . y^e . Coffee.
   Hand holding coffee-pot.
   Rev.   Hovse . in . Fryday . Street.
   [16]71.—1^d.
   A fine specimen of the large brass
   size.

   Sam. Watson. — Hand pouring
   coffee into a cup.
   Rev.   In . Fryday . Streete = His
   half peny.

GILTSPUR STREET.
   *Richard . Patricke . att . ye . his .
   ½.*—Turk's head.
   Rev.   *In . Giltspur . Street . w^{th}.
   out . Newgate . 1664.*

GRACECHURCH STREET.
   * New . Coffee . House . Hall.—
   A dog.
   Rev.   In . Grace . Church . Street.
   —T. D. and N.B. conjoined .
   1^d.

When rebuilt this street was commonly named as above, having
been previously called Gracious
Street (from the Grass market).
However the form of the name affords no clue to the exact date of
the token.   As early as 1320 (in a
letter book, quoted by Wheatley),
we have *Gras cherche* Street: in
Stow's Survey (ed. of 1598, p. 148),
it is written *Grasse streete :* Ogilby's
map, published subsequently to the
fire, gives it as *Gratious Street.* The
brass tokens, of which this is a
small example, are numerous and

in good preservation. Some of the earlier specimens were inscribed with this plea, *though I'm but brass, yet let me pass!*

*GRAY FRIARS, NEWGATE STREET.
Richard . Tart . in . Gray .— Coffee-man filling coffee-cup.
Rev. Friers . his . half . peny.— R.T.

HOLBORN.
At . yᵉ . Coffe . Hovse . against— Henry Mvscvt.—A hand holding cup.
Rev. Brook . Hovse . in . Holborn . his . half . peny. H.E.M.

There is a specimen of the above in the British Museum. Like a few others of this period, it was heart-shaped ; another variety of token was the diamond shape.

IRONMONGER LANE.
Richard . Askew.—Coffee-pot.
Rev. Ironmvnger . Lane. — R.A.A.

KING STREET, WESTMINSTER.
* Edward Barnard at yᵉ Dolphin in King Street, in Westminster.
Rev. A dolphin : below, hand pouring coffee.—His half peny.
Dr. Edw. Lake in his diary (Camden Society, No. 39), mentions the Romer in King Street [? Westminster], having just before, under date of December 11, 1677, spoken of discourse held 'at the R. coffee-house.' The famous Rummer Tavern was situate near Charing Cross.

LAD LANE.
Iohn . Marsh . 1669.—Table with three coffee-cups and a hand holding coffee-pot.
Rev. In . Lad . Lane.—His half peny.

LAWRENCE LANE, CHEAPSIDE.
Carlille . in . 1671.—Turk's head.
Rev. Lavrence . Lane.—A monogram.

LEADENHALL STREET.
Near . the . East . India . Hovs . —Turk's head.
Rev. In . Leadenhall . Street.— Iohns half peny.
See Muddiman's list, *Appendix F.*

LOTHBURY.
* At . the . West . Cvntry . Coffe. —I.S.
Rev. Hovse . in . Lothebvry.— Hand pouring coffee.

At . the . Turkes . Head.— Turk's head.
Rev. In . Loathbvry . 1659.— R.A.R.
This is the earliest date actually inscribed on a Coffee House Token, though there are tokens of the year 1648. In round numbers, of the eighty London Coffee House Tokens that are known to collectors, some thirty have the sign of a Turk's head.
No. XVI. of *Select City Quaeries for* 1660, refers to 'their selling of coffee and other cordial liquors' at the Turk's Head *by London Wall.*

LUDGATE WITHIN.
Thos . Strovd . at.—Turk's head.
Rev. Lvdgate . Coffee . Hovse. —A view of Ludgate.

MINORIES.
* Henry . Sadd . in . yᵉ . Minoryes.— H.S. and a crowned rose.
Rev. A . Coffe . Halfe . penny. [16]66.—Turk's head and H.S.

NEW STREET, COVENT GARDEN.
Ioseph.—A man holding cup

into which a hand pours coffee from a coffee-pot: table on which are three pipes.

Rev. Howard . Coffe . Hovse . in . New . Street . 1671.

A variety in the British Museum has only two pipes on the table.

OLD JEWRY.
* Robins in Old Iewry. — The figure 3, in indentation.
Rev. Blank.

A leather token. In the British Museum there is a duplicate and another specimen having the figure 4.

PANIER ALLEY.
* Robert . Hayes . at . ye . Coffe.
—Turk's head.
Rev. Hovse . in . Panier . Alley.
—His half peny.

Hayes being burnt out moved to Barbican, where he issued another and more carefully executed token. In 1675 one *Hayes* kept a Coffee House in Paternoster Row.

PATERNOSTER ROW.
* Chapter Coffe House (4).—A mitre.
Rev. Blank.

A leather groat. Another different and smaller in size, but also leather and gilded; see Illustration. Two more, one of leather and the other of pewter,[1] are in the British Museum. In the first of these tokens and in the last, all the letters and the figures are reversed.

RATCLIFFE HIGHWAY,
* Will . Archer at . the.—Hand, with coffee-pot.
Rev. Coffe . Hovse . in . Ratlefe.
— His half peny.

RUSSELL STREET, COVENT GARDEN.
Timothy . Child . at . ye . Coffe.
—Turk's head.
Rev. Hovse . in . Rvssell . Street.
= His halfe peny.

* Mary Long in Russell.—A rose on stem.
Rev. Street in Covent Garden.
—Her halfe penny, M.L.

Mary Long was the widow of William Long, and her initials, together with those of her husband, appear on a token issued from the Rose Tavern in Bridge Street, Covent Garden.

Tickets for the Mathematical Adventure, 'a lottery to be drawn at Stationers' hall,' were announced in *The Post-boy* newspaper, Feb. 25, 1698-9, as obtainable at 'the Rose Coffee House, by the playhouse' [Burn]. Will's Coffee House, at the corner of Russell Street and Bow Street, at one time had the sign of the rose.

Pet . Spitster . in . Rvsel.—Turk's head.
Rev. Street . in . Coven . Garden = His half peny.

There is a mention of *Peter's* Coffee House in the *State Trials*, Hargrave, 1683.

* ST. ANN'S LANE, ALDERSGATE STREET.
Nich . Strainge . at . ye . Coffee.
—Turk's head.
Rev. Hovse . in . St . Anns . Lane . [16]69.—Hand pouring coffee.

---

[1] A truly quaint specimen; its lettering is in part upside down and the *Rev.* blank.

ST. BRIDE'S.
William . Norse . in . St.—Turk's
head.
Rev. Brides . Chvrch . Yard =
Coffee Hovse.

ST. CLEMENT'S.
Christopher . Danbrook.— Hand
pouring coffee into cup.
Rev. In . St . Clements . Lane
= His half peny.
Y᷄ . Coffee . Hovse . against.—
W.E.S.
Rev. St . Clements . Church .
Strand.—His halfe peny.
**Abraham . Jorden . at . y*᷄ *. his .*
½ᵈ.—Turk's head.
Rev. behind . St . Clement .
Church . 1664.

ST. MARTIN'S LE GRAND.
Thomas . Jackson . in . St. Mar-
tins Le . grand.—his Peny.
Rev. In . Kings . Head . Covrt.
—Table with two cups, into
one of which a hand is pouring.
See Muddiman's list, *Appendix*
F.

ST. MICHAEL'S ALLEY.
Stephen . Hayward . Geo. . Back-
ler.—Hand pouring coffee.
Rev. At . the . Ovld . Coffee .
Hovse . in . St. Michaells . Ally . formerly . Bomans . ½.
This interesting token is in the
British Museum.
Houghton (here quoted from
Douglas, but see also Appendix B)
says, 'Bowman died in 1663, and
after one year his wife left the house
to one *Batler*, whose daughter
married Humphry Hodskins, Bowman's second Apprentice, who was
with him before Monk's March in
1659.'

ST. PAUL'S CHURCHYARD.
* The . Coffe . Hovse . at the.—
Turk's head.

Rev. West . End of . St . Pavls .
London.—E.W.B. in a mono-
gram (reads equally well inverted).
See *Appendix F* for a mention
of Child from whom the Coffee
House was named. It was, like 'the
Chapter,' a convenient resort for the
clergy, and was afterwards visited
by the Royal Society Club (see
Timbs' Clubs, pp. 56. 345). See
under *Russell Street* for Timothy
Child.

SCALDING ALLEY, POULTRY.
Iohn . Landsdell.—Hand pour-
ing coffee.
Rev. In . Scalding . Alley.—
His half peny.

SHOE LANE, FLEET STREET.
* Mansfields . Coffee . Hovse.—
Hand holding coffee-pot.
Rev. In . Shoe . Lane . by .
Providence.—[?] A column be-
tween two coffee-cups and
pipes.

SMITHFIELD.
* At . the . Harts . Horns . in .
West.—Sultan's head.
Rev. Smithfeild . the . Coffe .
hovs.—C.M.C. ½ token . 1664.
Burn quotes from the *Mercurius*
Politicus, June 24, 1658, an announcement that, ' on and after the 28th,
all persons having occasion to travel
fr. London to Manchester,' &c.,
might obtain ' a good and able
single horse, or more, furnished,
at three-pence a mile, without
charge of a guide, by applying to
Mr. Christopher Charteris [see his
initials above] at the sign of the
Hart's Horns, in West Smithfield. '

SPITALFIELDS.
Ralph . Wilkes . in.—His halfe
peny.

Rev. Spittle . Feilds . at . the.
—Bust of a Turk holding cup.

A second token has the initials R.R.W. in the field.

The *frontispiece* represents a sign in tiles which, as Mr. James Smith, an old collector, well remembers, was formerly in Baxter's Coffee Rooms, No. 66, Brick Lane, Spital-fields. The house in question was ancient, and possessed a single bay window. The tiling was let into the right hand wall, at a height of about five feet from the ground, and was opposite to the wooden seats provided for customers just *inside* the first room. The design is in blue on a white ground, the hair of the boy and the heel of his shoe being coloured red. The pipes probably belong to the Restoration period, if we may judge from similar specimens preserved in the Guildhall Museum; other accessories point in the same direction. Only a part of the tiling is preserved, and of this one small piece is inverted.

STAR COURT.
At . the   Coffee . Hovse . in.—
Hand pouring coffee.
Rev.   Star . Covrt . Bread .
Street.—A star.

STRAND.
Richard . Lione . in . y^e . Strand.
Rev.   His . half . peny.—A lion rampant pouring out a cup of coffee.

See under *Warwick Lane.*

SWEETING'S RENTS, CORNHILL.
* The . Svltaness . a . Coffee .
Hovse —A veiled head.
Rev.   In . Sweetings . Rents .
Cornhil.   Heraldic device.

See page 126 for an early advertisement of this house.

THREADNEEDLE STREET.
W^m. Stonyer . his . ½ peney.—
Turk's head.
Rev.   Ag^t . y^e . French . Chvrch .
in . Thred . Nedle . Street.

There are two specimens in the British Museum, the die of the second is slightly varied.

TOOLEY STREET.
Ed. Orpin at Coffe Hovse.—An angel.
Rev.   In Tooley Streete 1666.—
His half peny.

TOWER ROYAL.
* *Tho. Scarlett . his . Coffie .
Penny.*
Rev.   Neere . the . Tower . Royall.
—Turk's head.

* W. Shaw . at . the . Coffee.—
Hand holding coffee-pot.
Rev.   Hovse . in . Towre . Royal.
—W.F.S.

TOWER STREET.
William . Shears . in.—Hand holding cup : table on which are two cups.
Rev.   Tower . Street . 1669=A coffee penny.

LITTLE TRINITY LANE.
* Mary . Stringer . 1669.—Hand pouring coffee : tobacco-pipes on table.
Rev.   In . Little . Trinity . Lane
=Her half peny.

WARWICK LANE, NEWGATE ST.
*Richard . Lyon . in . Warwick .
Lane.*
Rev.   His . Half . Peny.—A lion rampant holding a coffee-pot.

———

UNIDENTIFIED.
A . Coffee . Peney . for.—Coffee pot and cups.
Rev.   Necessary . Change. — A stove.

Possibly issued after the Royal Proclamation, at the close of 1674, had enjoined the prosecution of any who should 'utter base metals with private stamps' or 'hinder the vending of those half-pence and farthings which are provided for necessary exchange.' See the whole proclamation as quoted by Burn (*Introd.* p. xl.).

DOUBTFUL.

Iohn . Tvrner . at . the.—Friar's head (?).
Rev. In . Chancery . Lane . 1668 = His halfe penny.—I.D.T.

There are many other tokens which do not give any clue to the trade of the issuer ; e.g. that put forth by Mary Long, in Russell Street.

PROVINCIAL COFFEE HOUSE TOKENS.

CAMBRIDGE.

Iohn . Marston . in . Trvmp.—A hand pouring coffee into one of four cups on a table.
Rev. ington street . Cambr . His halfe penny.—A rose.

The rose is a common design on the Cambridgeshire Tokens ; these extend from 1651 to 1671.

DUBLIN.

The . Coffee . House . in . Dublin.—Lionell Newman . 1664.

Williamson's Boyne gives as the reverse ' *Morat* '—a Turk's Head, and Dr. Aquila Smith, in his catalogue, gives ' A lion rampant.'

EXETER.

Achier . Brocas.—Turk's head.
Rev. In . Exon . 1607 [1667 ?] —A coffee pot.

A variety is spelt Achior and the coffee-pot is held by a hand.

OXFORD.

Lawrence . Short . neare.—Hand holding a coffee-pot.
Rev. New Colledg . in Oxon = L.E.S.

Of the tokens in the Fitz William Museum, Cambridge, only one is known to have been issued by a coffee man. The case is similar at Oxford ; however, there are five specimens of Short's Token in the Bodleian. For this information, and for an addition to the Bibliography, I would express my indebtedness to Mr. E. B. Nicholson.

The following list, though it makes no pretension to completeness, will show that Coffee Houses in the XVIIth century were by no means confined to London and the Universities. A Newcastle merchant purchased, in 1666, a Turkish prize ship laden with coffee. At the Dorchester Assize, in 1686, coffee is mentioned in the bill for attendance of ' Mr. Bragge, town clerk of Lynne.' Doughtie's Coffee House, Lynn Regis, Norfolk, is mentioned in the *London Gazette*, July 15–19, 1675. Dean Davies, at a later time (c. 1690), speaks of the Coffee Houses at Yarmouth and at Chester. Bennet's Coffee House, Plymouth, was well known in the year 1692.

INDEX TO COFFEE HOUSES.